THIS BOOK BELONGS TO

. . . .

FEATURING THE STUDENTS OF JAY HIGH SCHOOL

The Book of
ECLECTIC ART

a coloring book compilation of student designs

Edited by T.S. Dobson

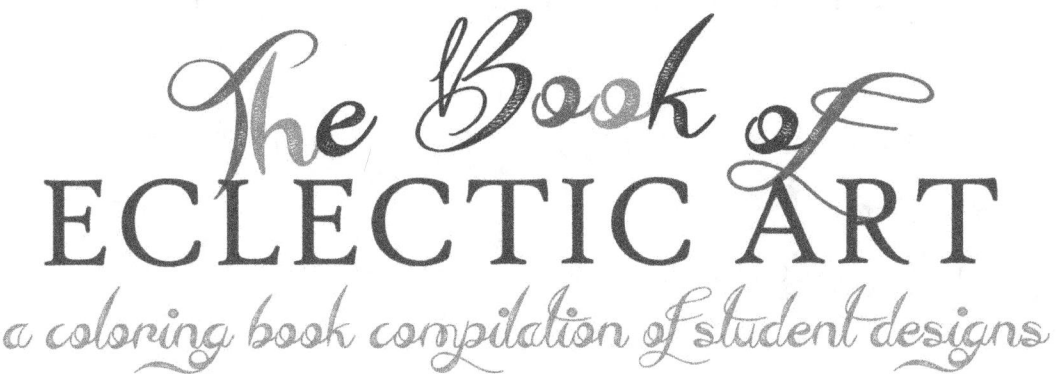

The Book of ECLECTIC ART
a coloring book compilation of student designs

Copyright 2018 by Jay High School

ISBN-13: 978-1717170743
ISBN-10: 1717170749

Cover Art by: Paisley Simmons

Instructor/Editor and Illustrator Teresa Scott Dobson

Back cover preview art created by students: Top Left— Jozey Lewis-Boutwell; Top Right— Samantha Westwood; Bottom Left— Tara Nevels; Bottom Right— Olivia Watson

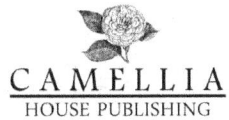

CAMELLIA
HOUSE PUBLISHING

Camellia House Publishing, Century, FL
Printed in the United States of America.

camelliahousepublishing@aol.com

BEFORE YOU GET STARTED!

1. Put away all of the worldly distractions around you -- TV, phone, computer, etc.

2. Take out some color pencils, markers or crayons.

3. Pick a page and go with it. There's no particular order to follow.

4. When you finish a design, personalize it by signing your name anywhere on the page.

5. Stop when you need a break, then pick it up again later.

6. When finished, if you desire, share your creations with others!

7. Enjoy the extra blank sheets and do your own designs at the back of the book.

8. One more important tip… make sure to place a blank sheet of paper in between the page designs as you color to cut down on ink bleed.

ENJOY!

On behalf of the Jay High School Art Department we appreciate your purchase of our diverse collection of young artists' works.

All proceeds go back to the Jay High School Art Department to help with the purchase of art supplies for our students.

We would love to see any of your finished creations! Send a picture of your art to *royalmandala@aol.com or visit us on Facebook and upload your art to Royal Mandala!* (Attach jpeg files 10 megs or less per email)

"Every child is an artist. The problem is how to remain an artist once we grow up."

Pablo Picasso

The Book of ECLECTIC ART

a coloring book compilation of student designs

TABLE OF CONTENTS BY ARTIST:

The Book of ECLECTIC ART

a coloring book compilation of student designs

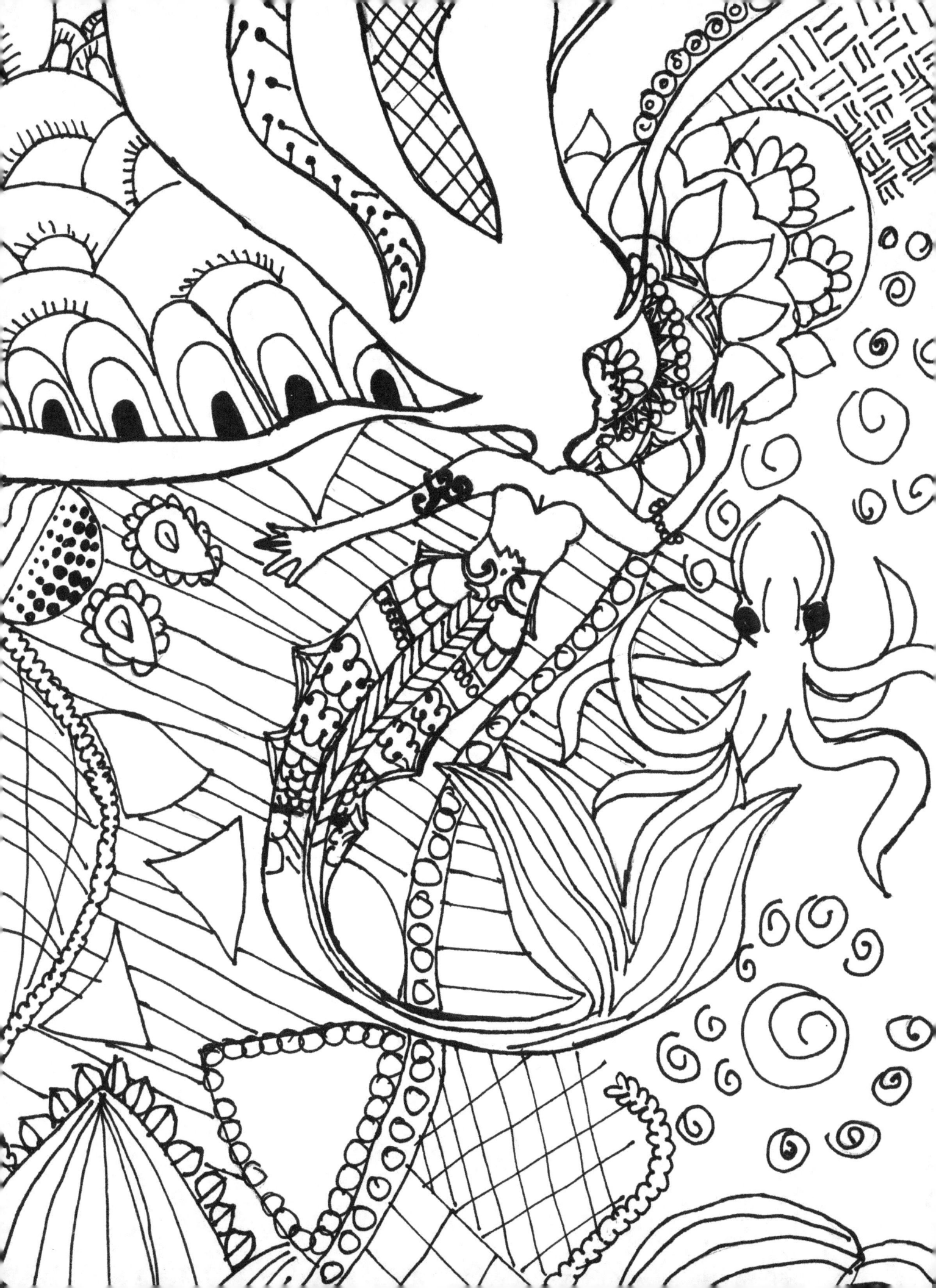

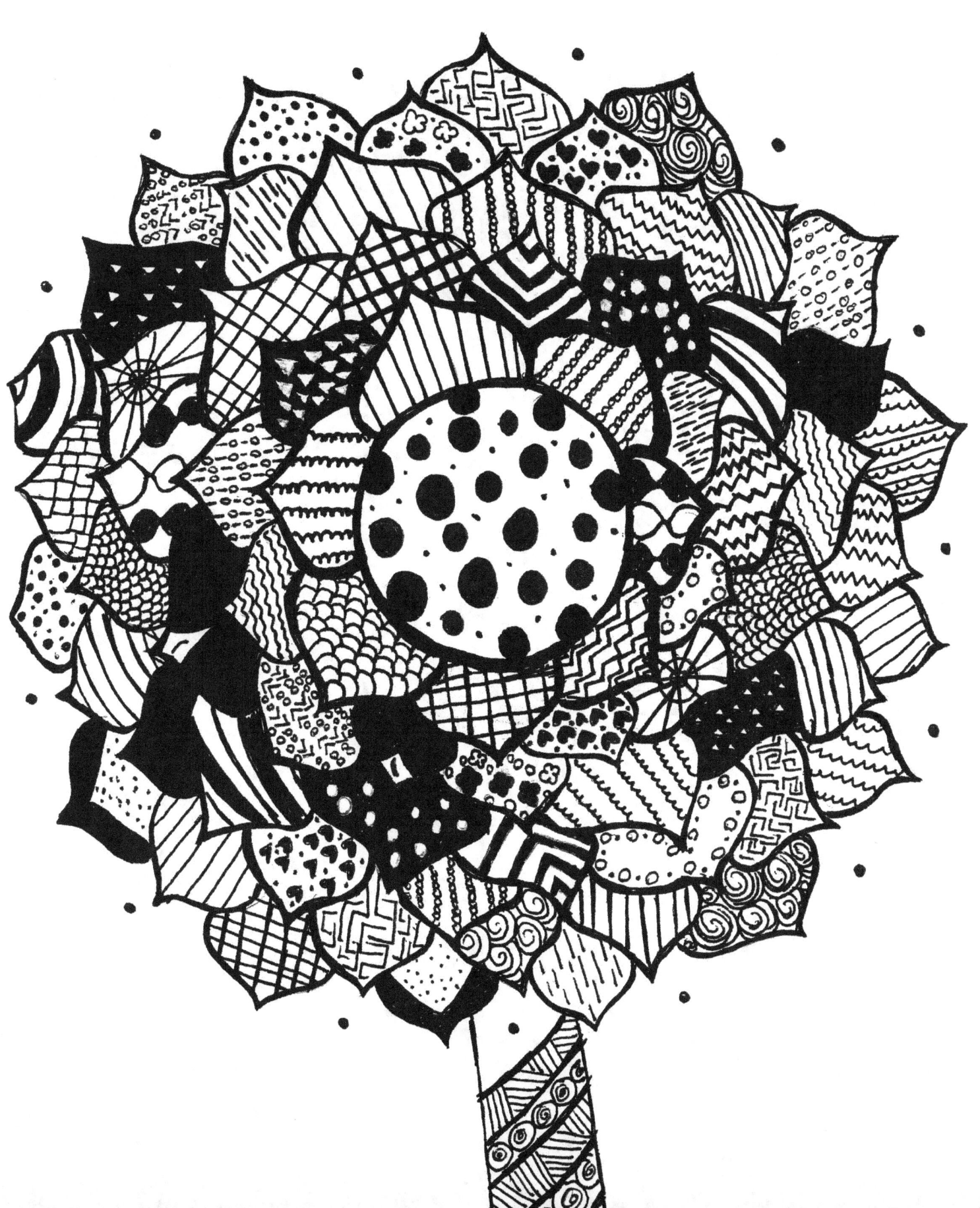

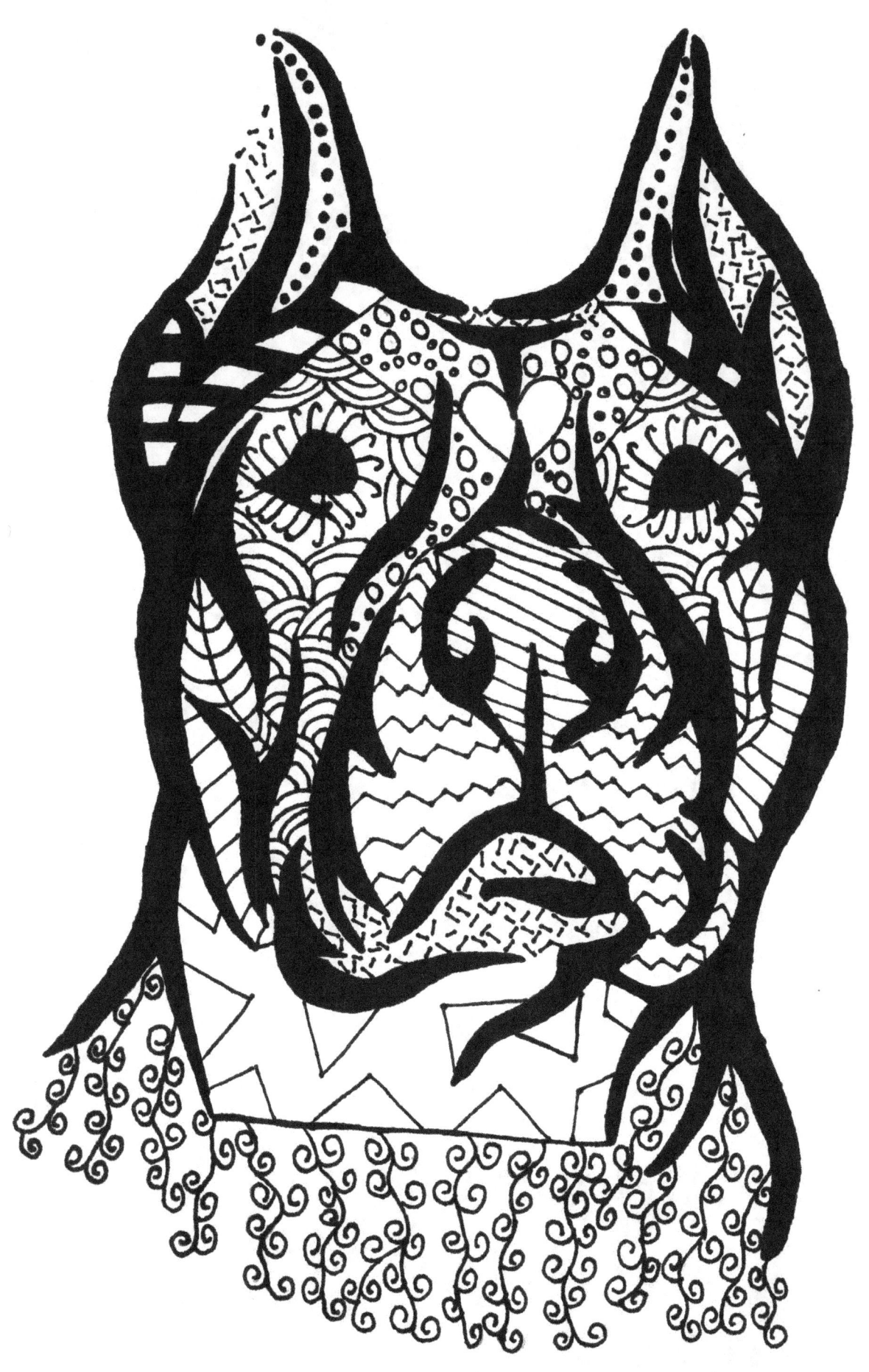

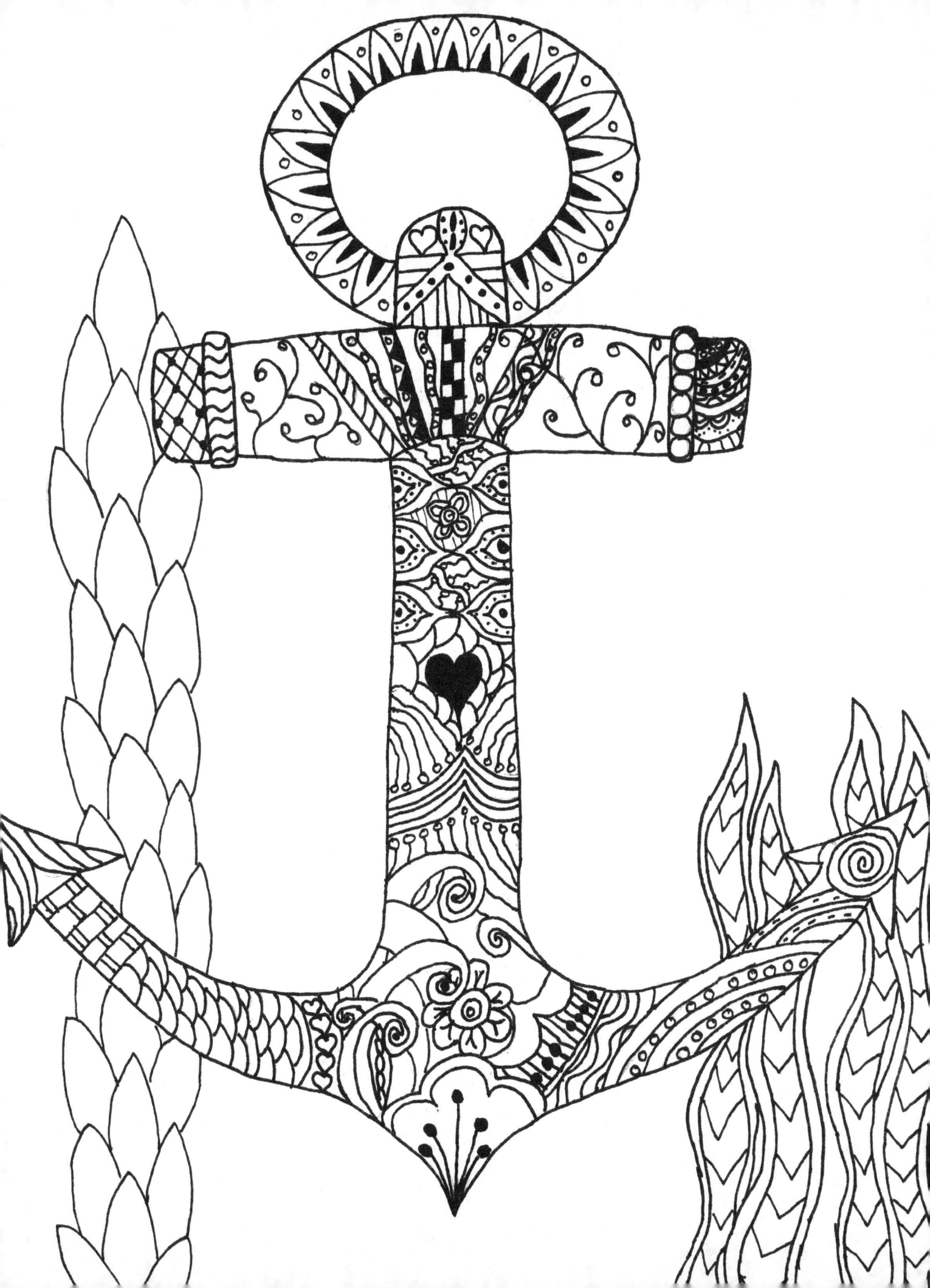

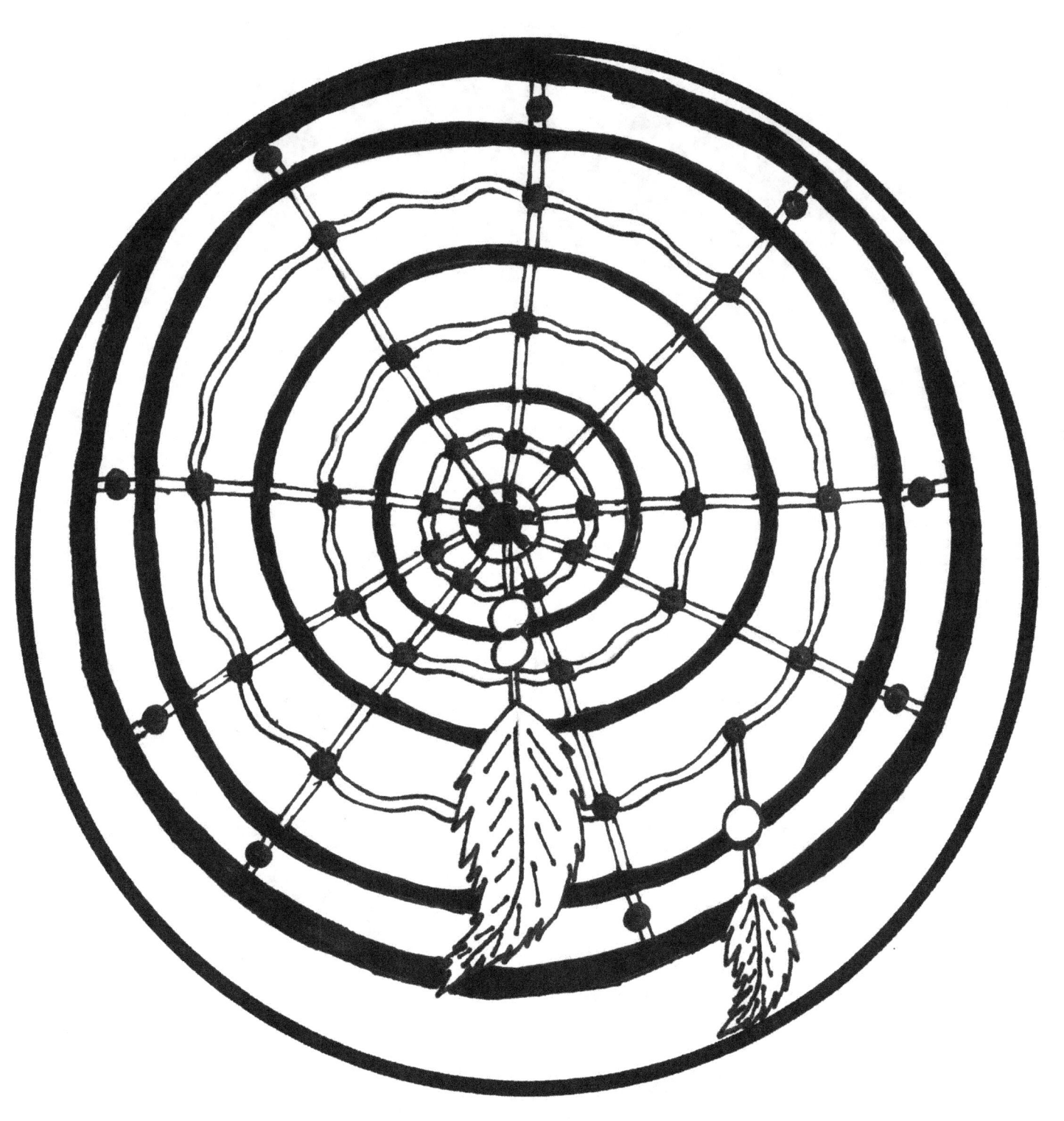

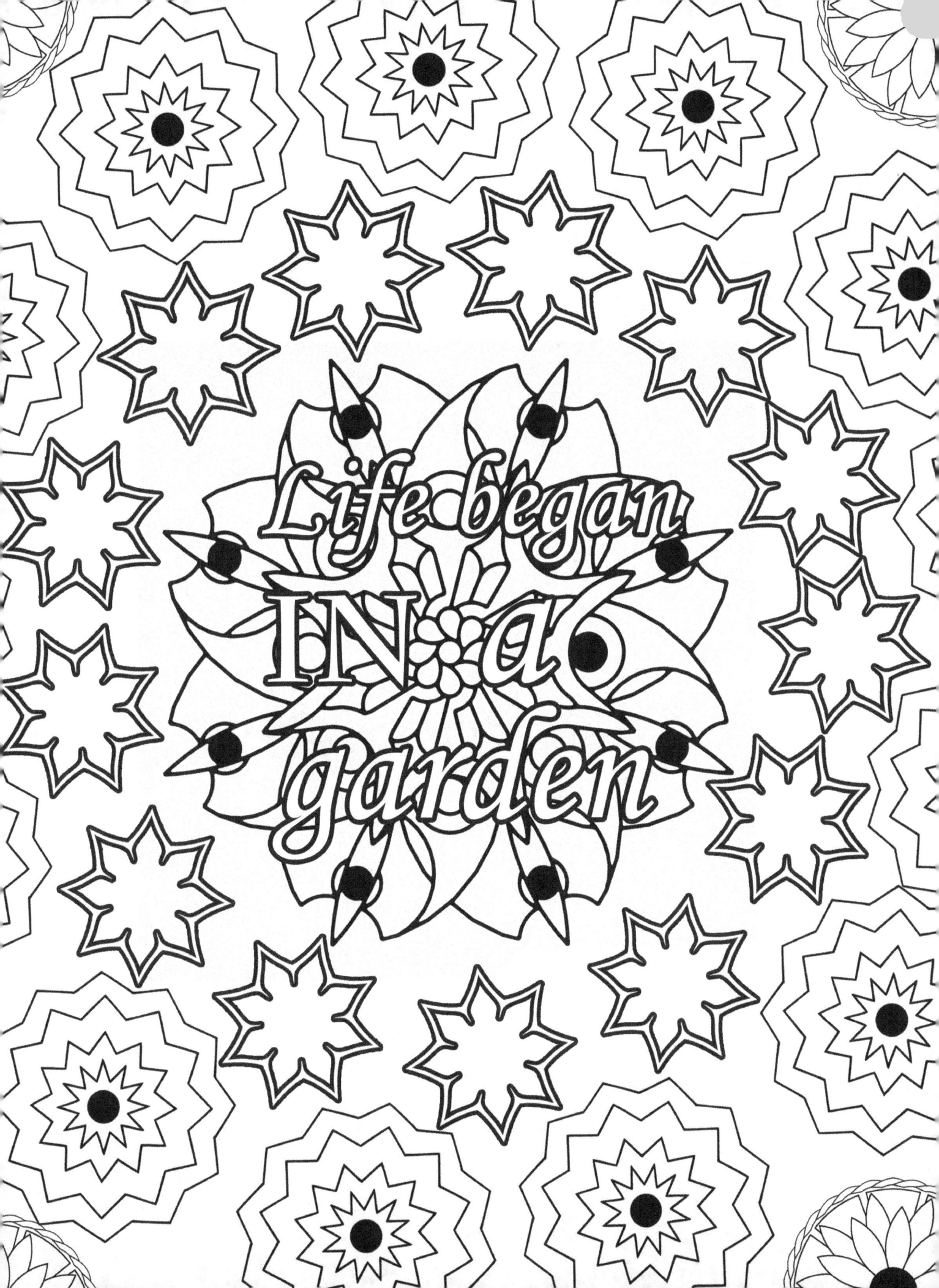

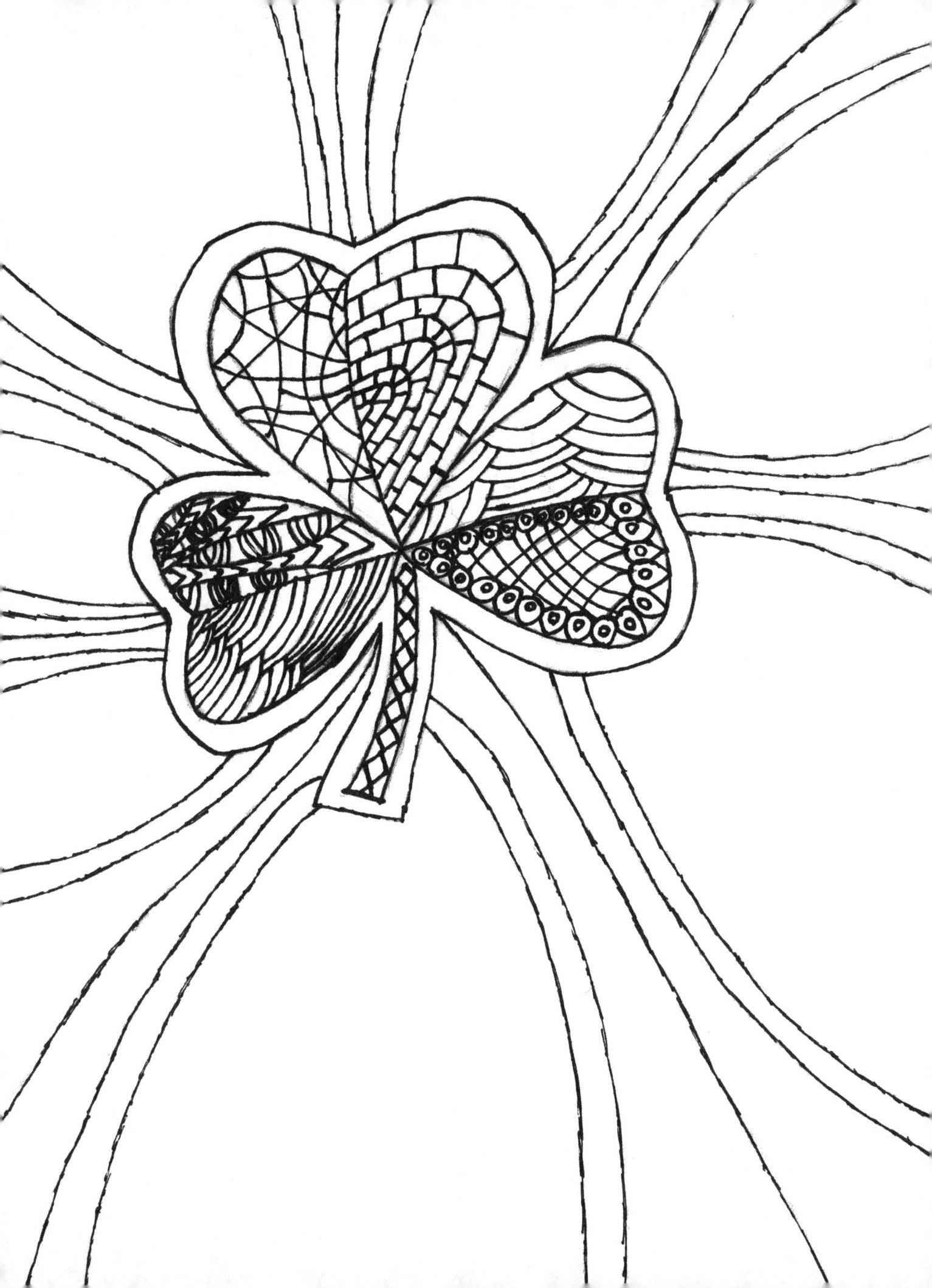

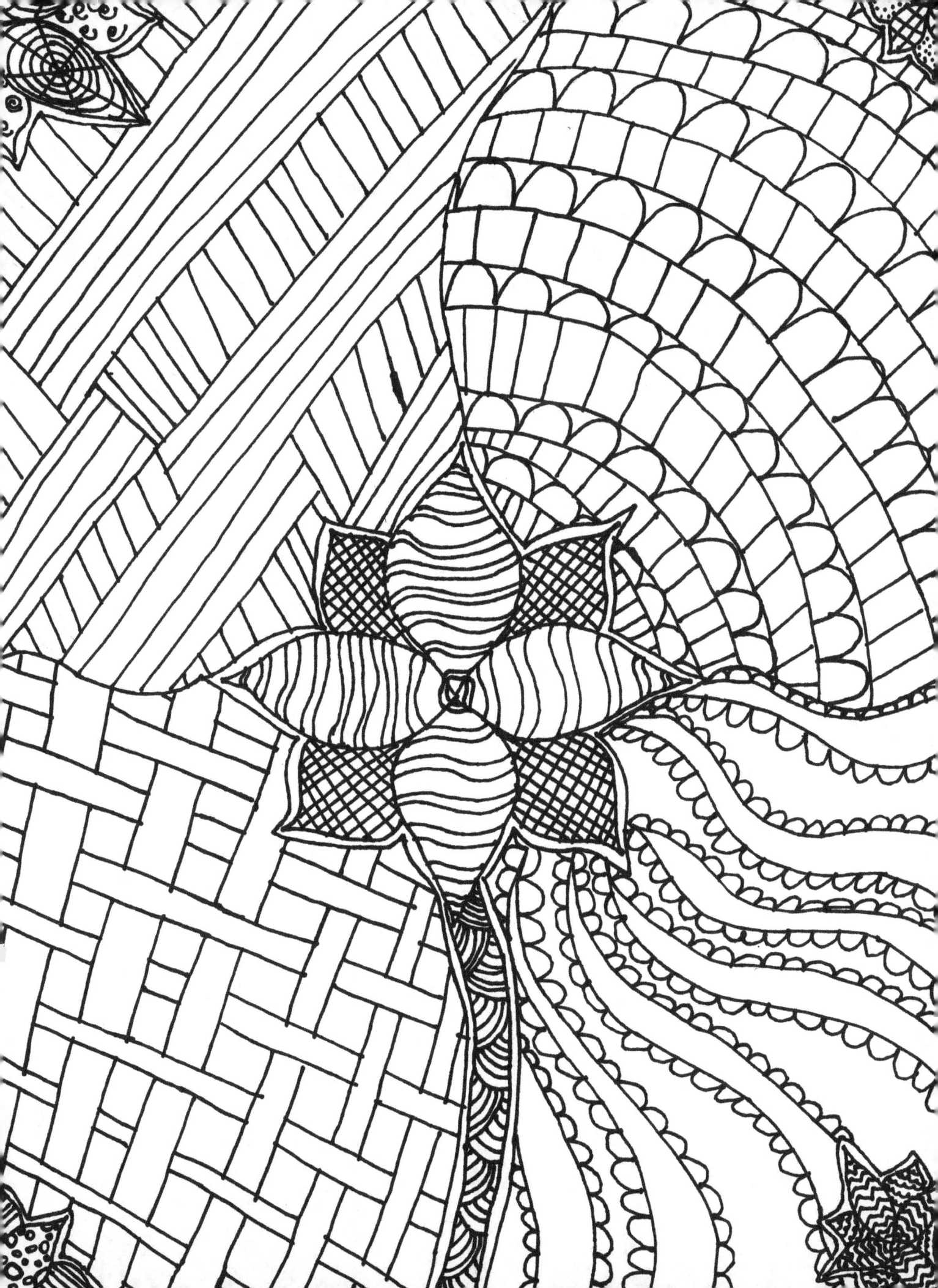

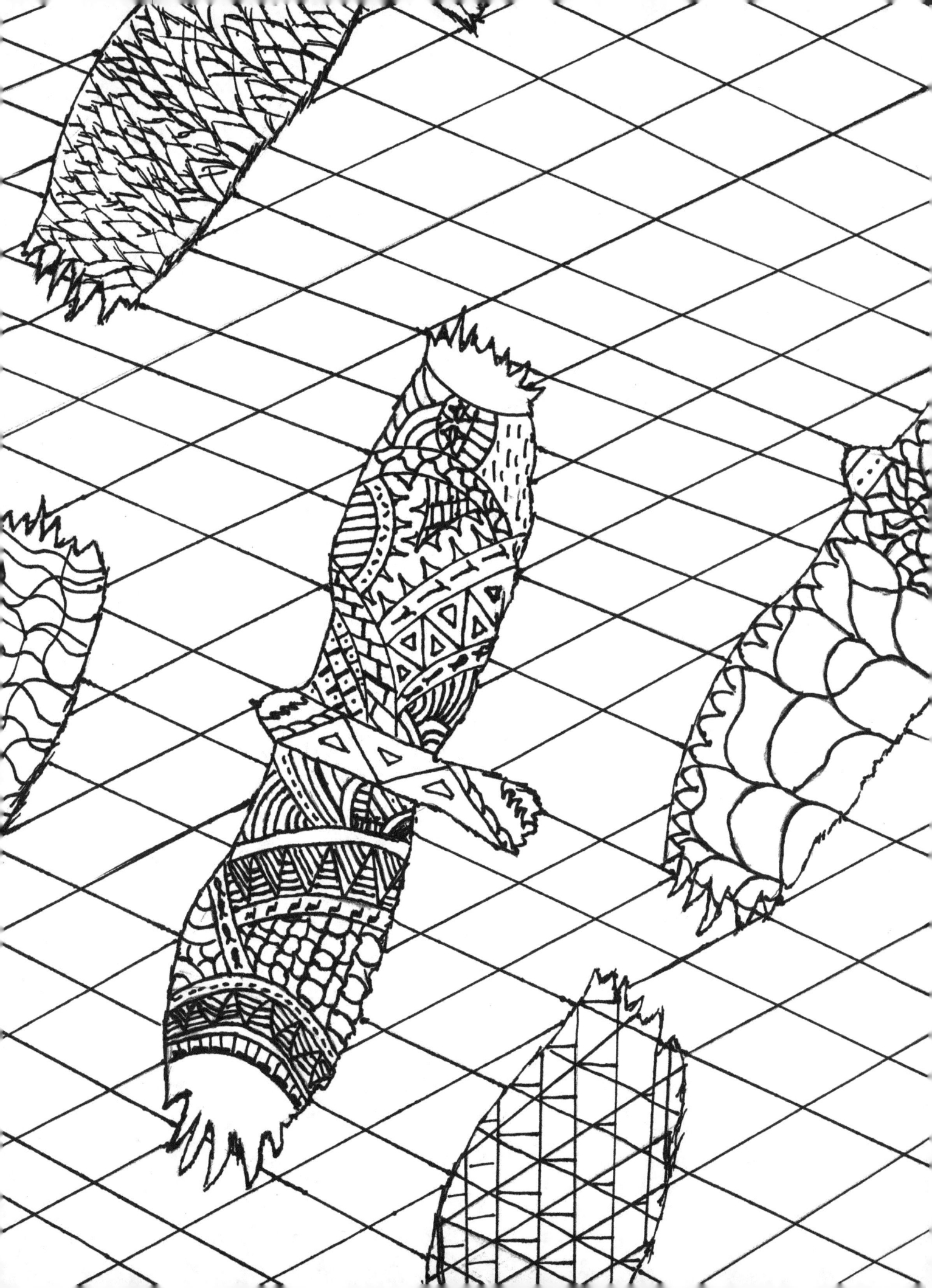

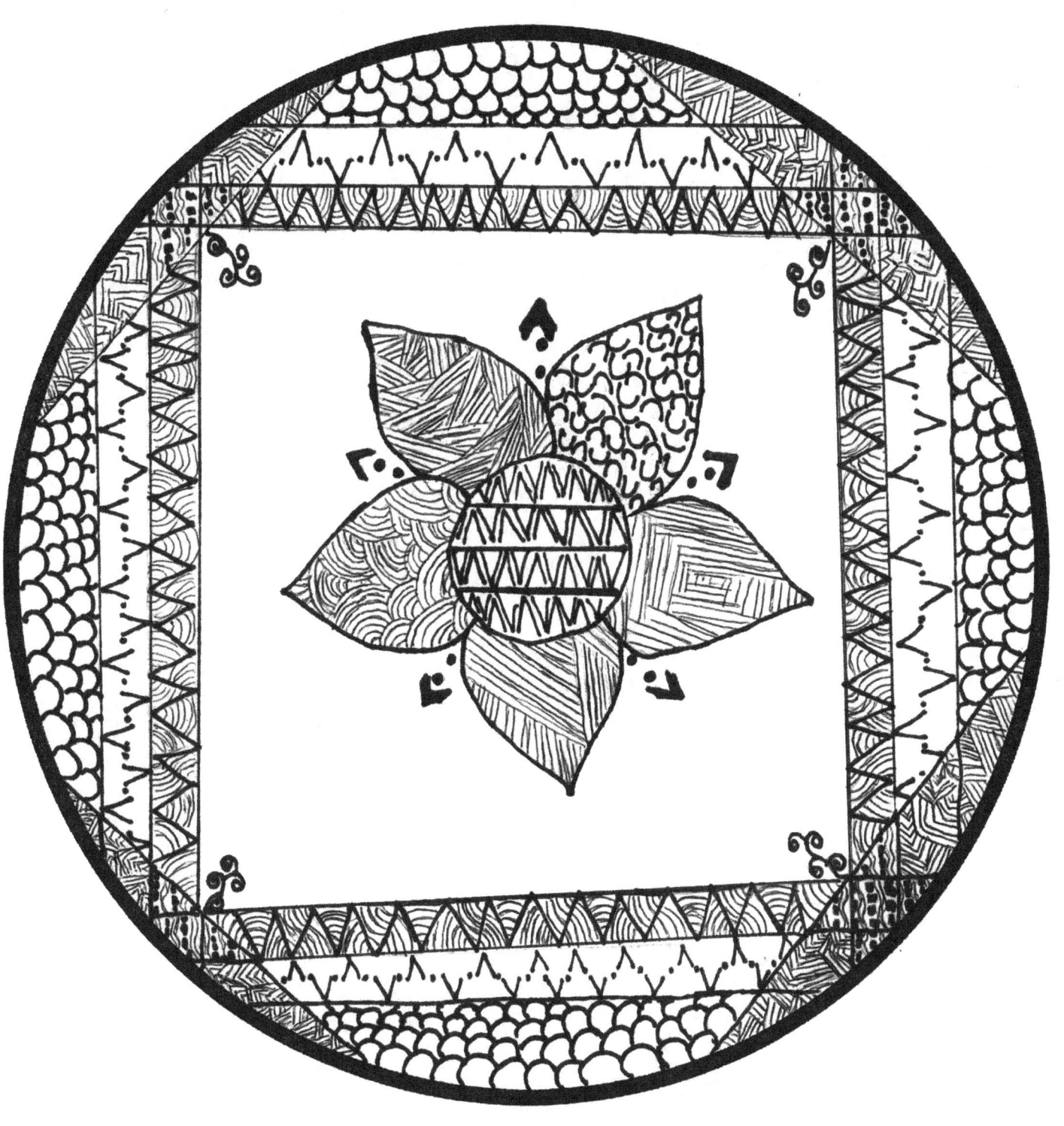

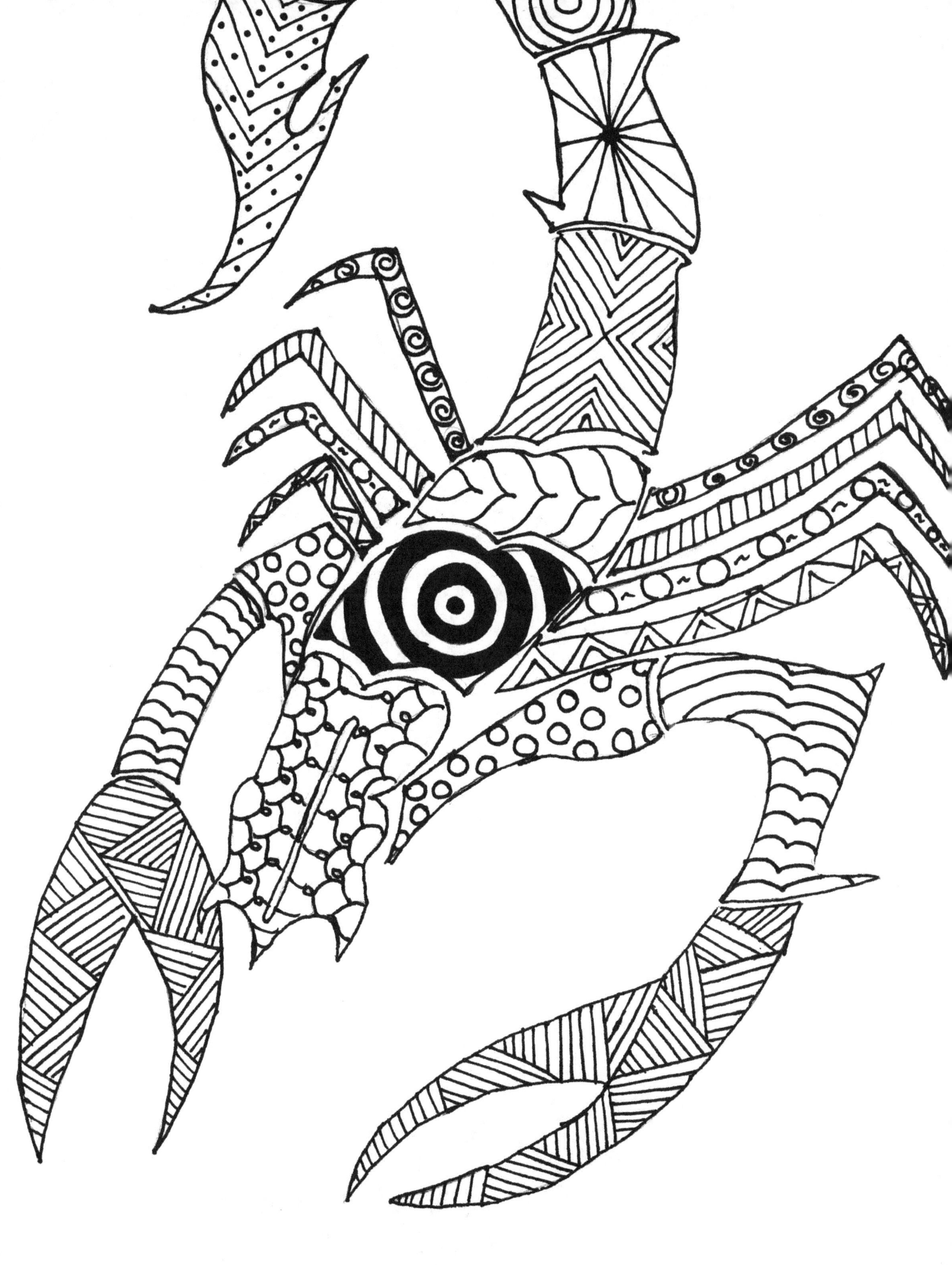

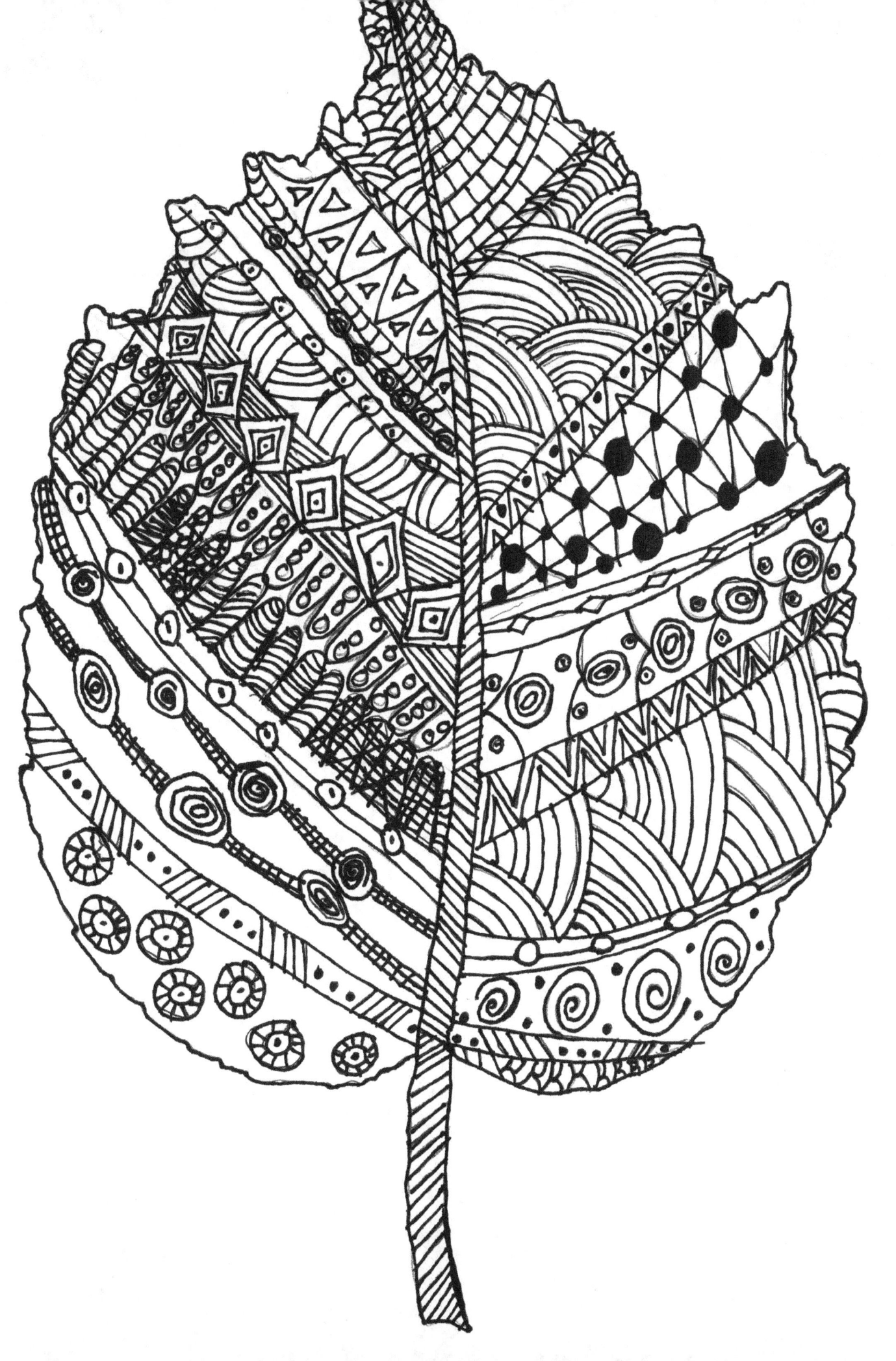

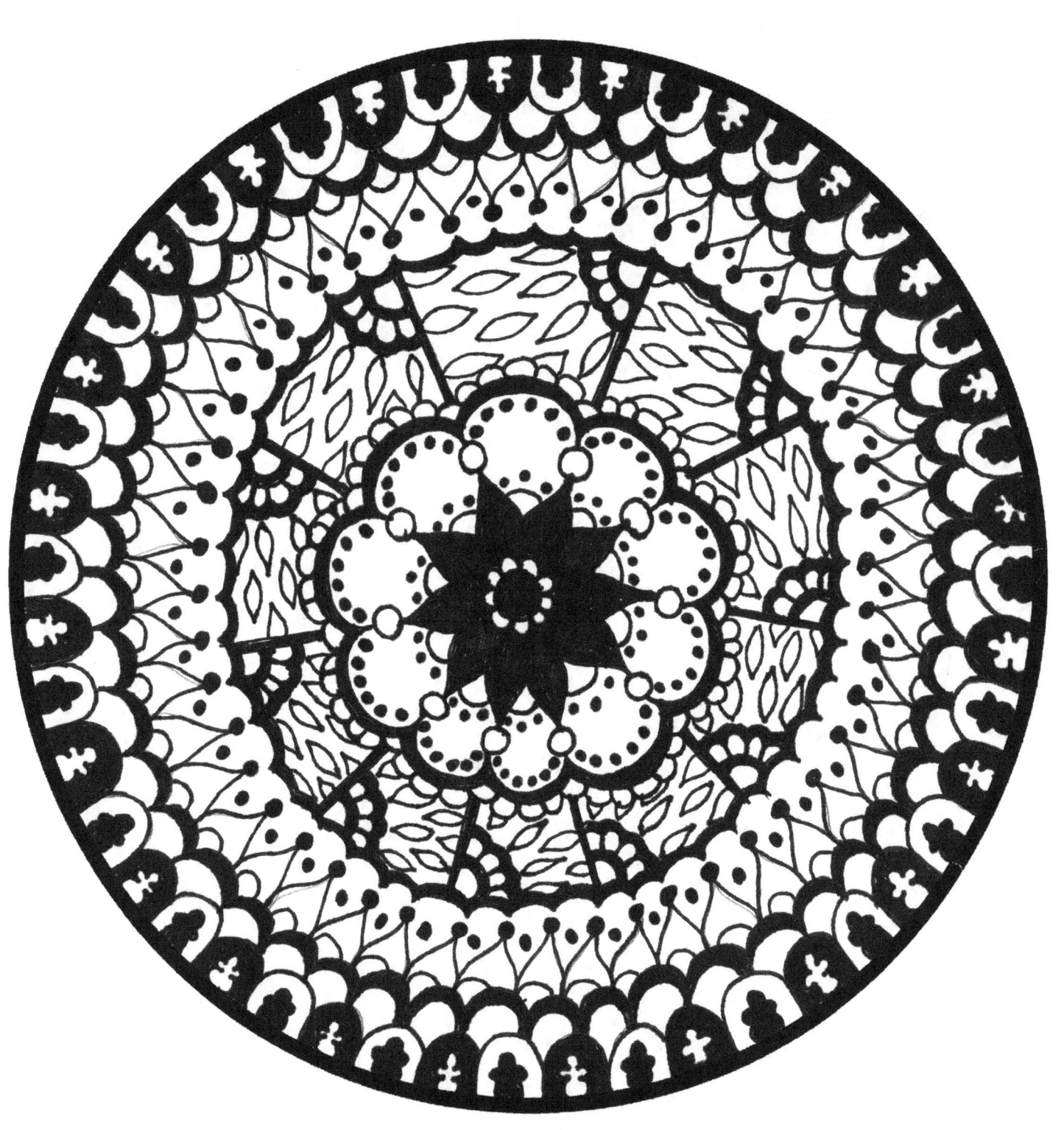

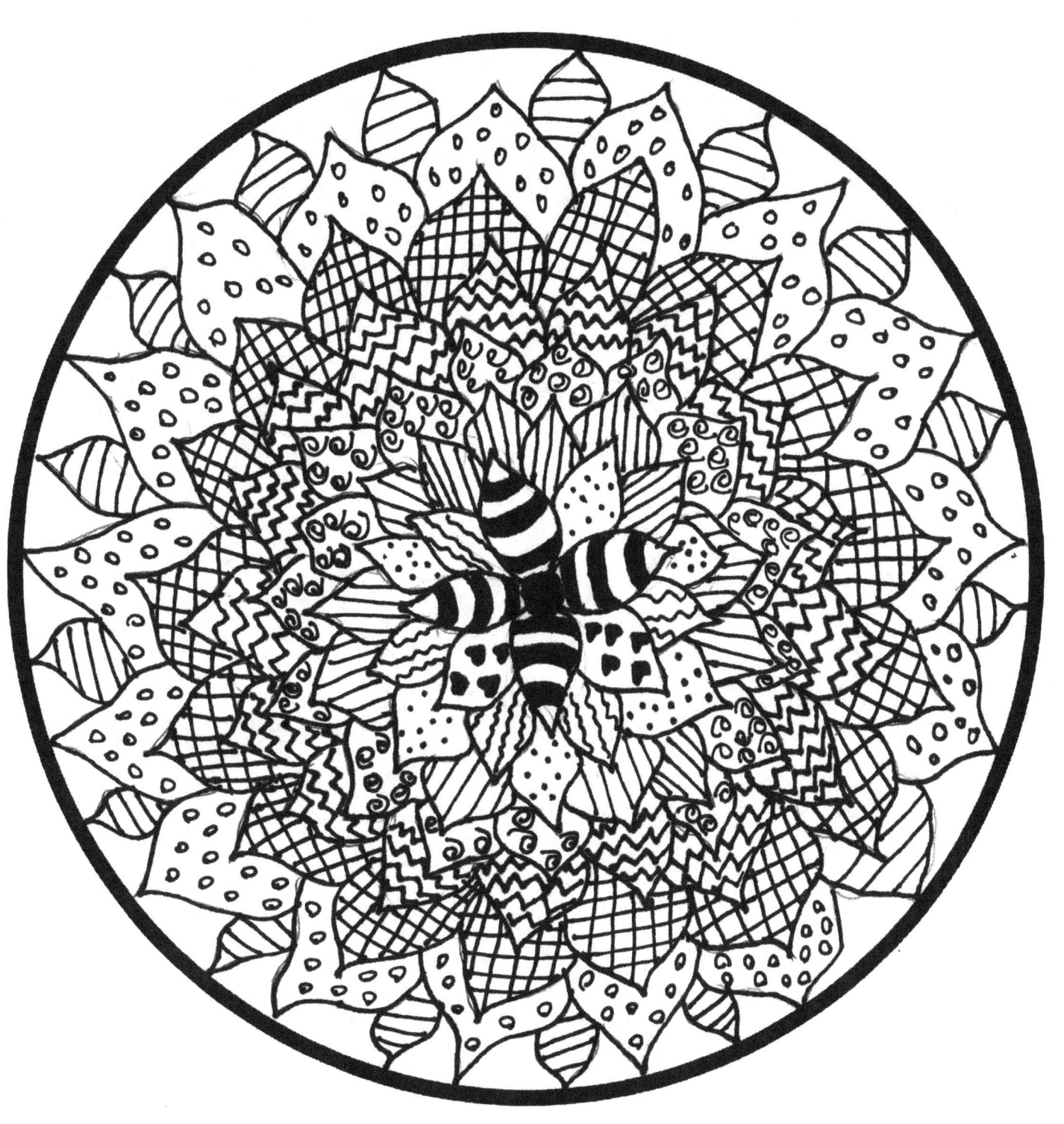

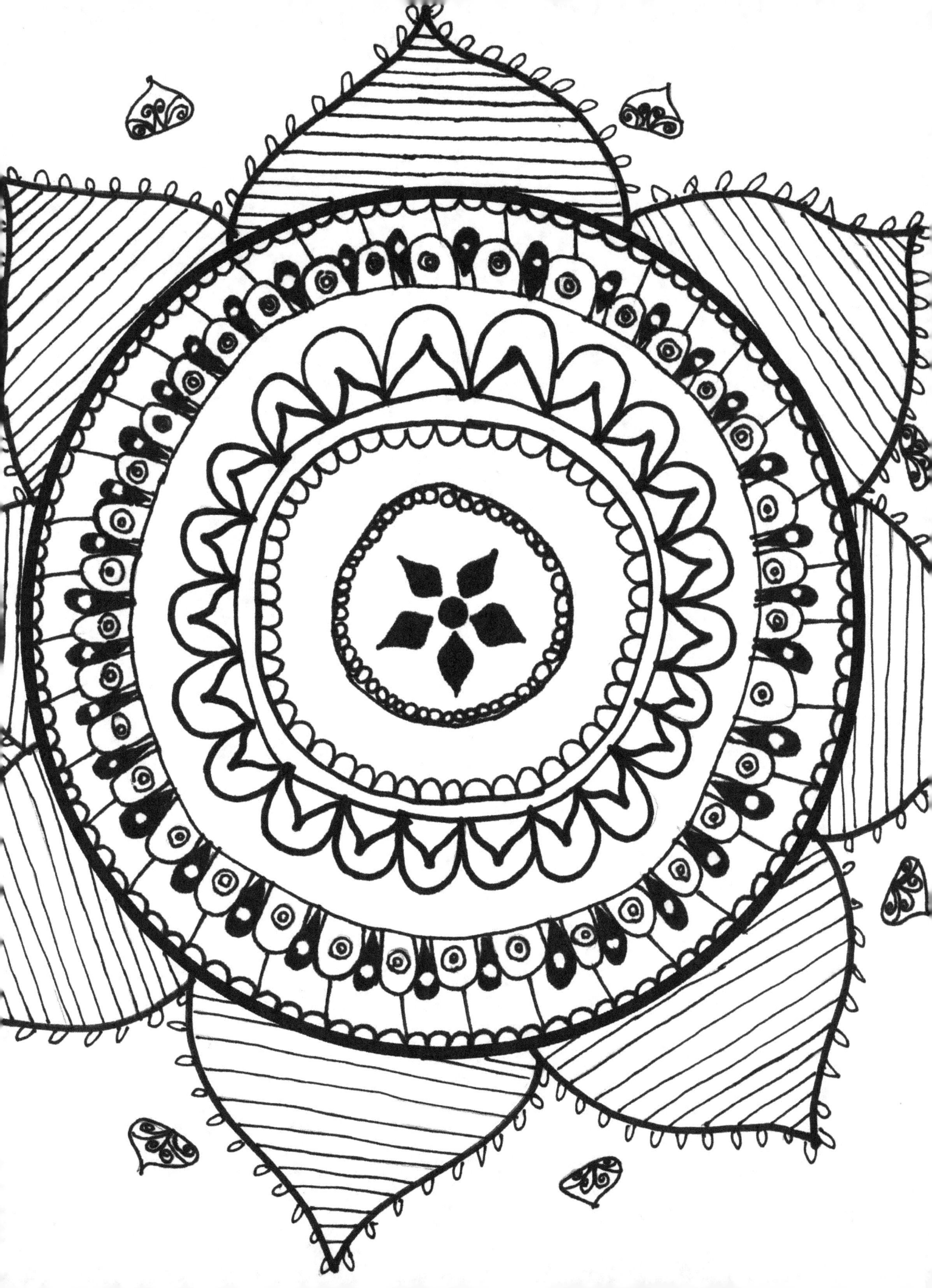

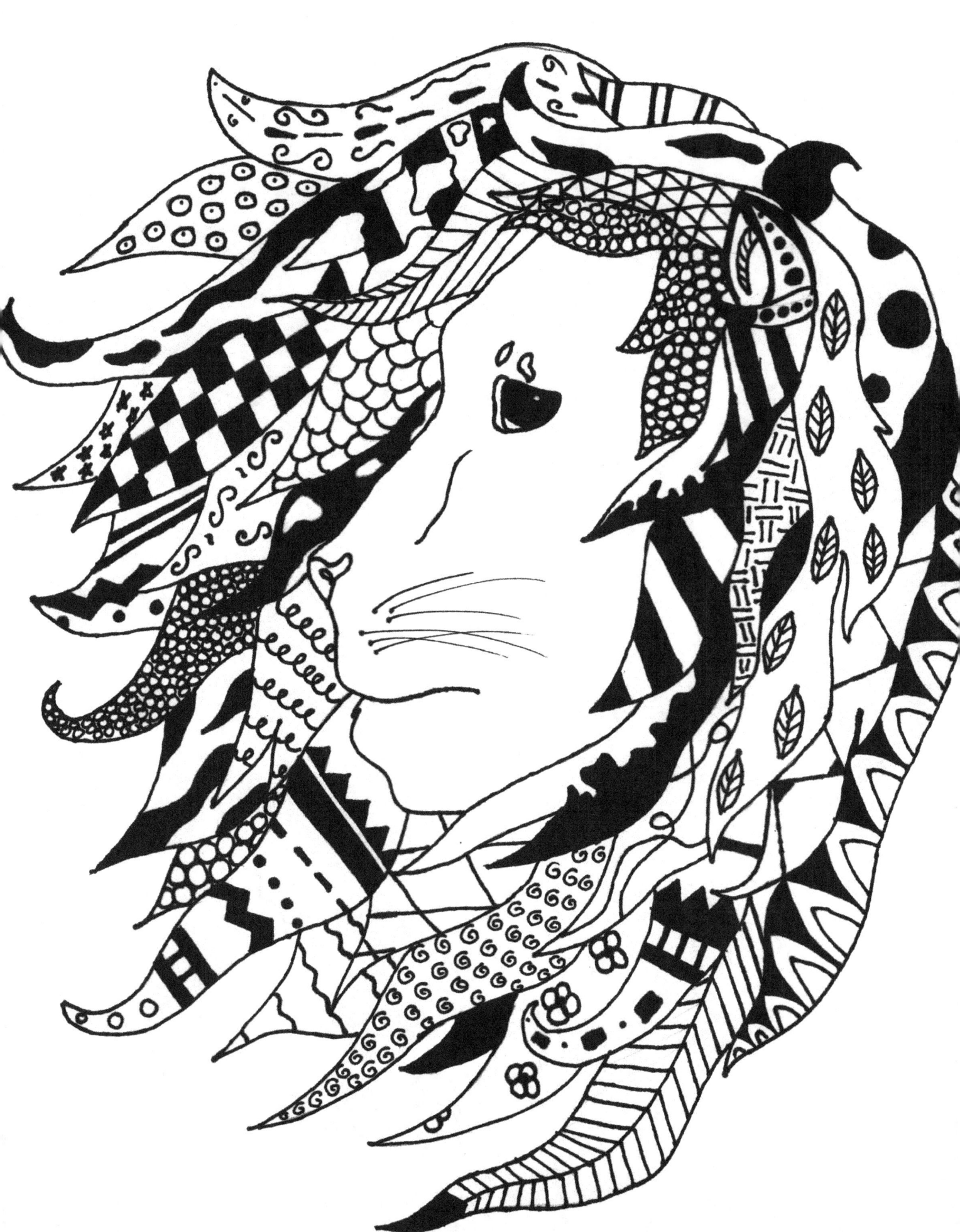

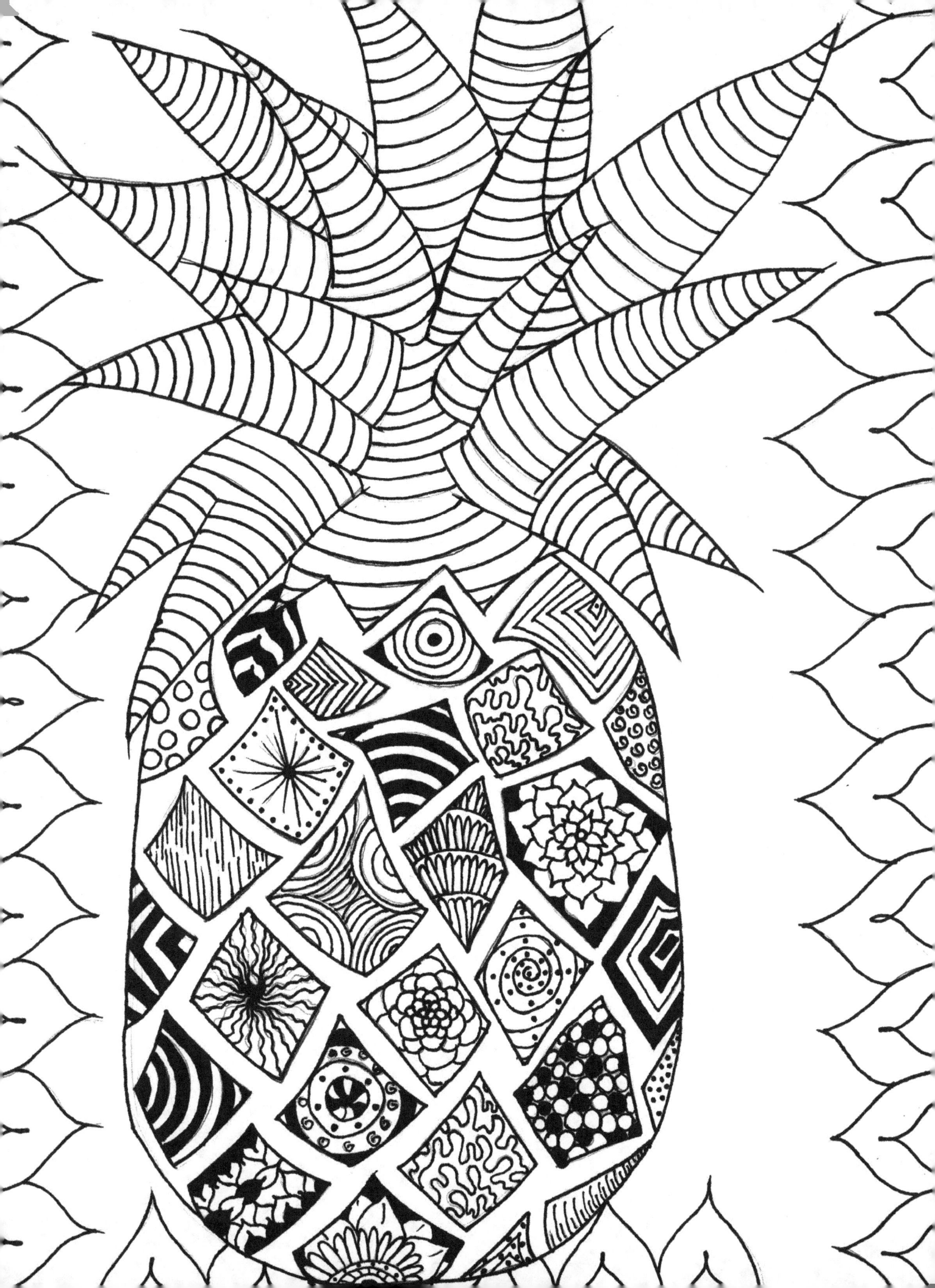

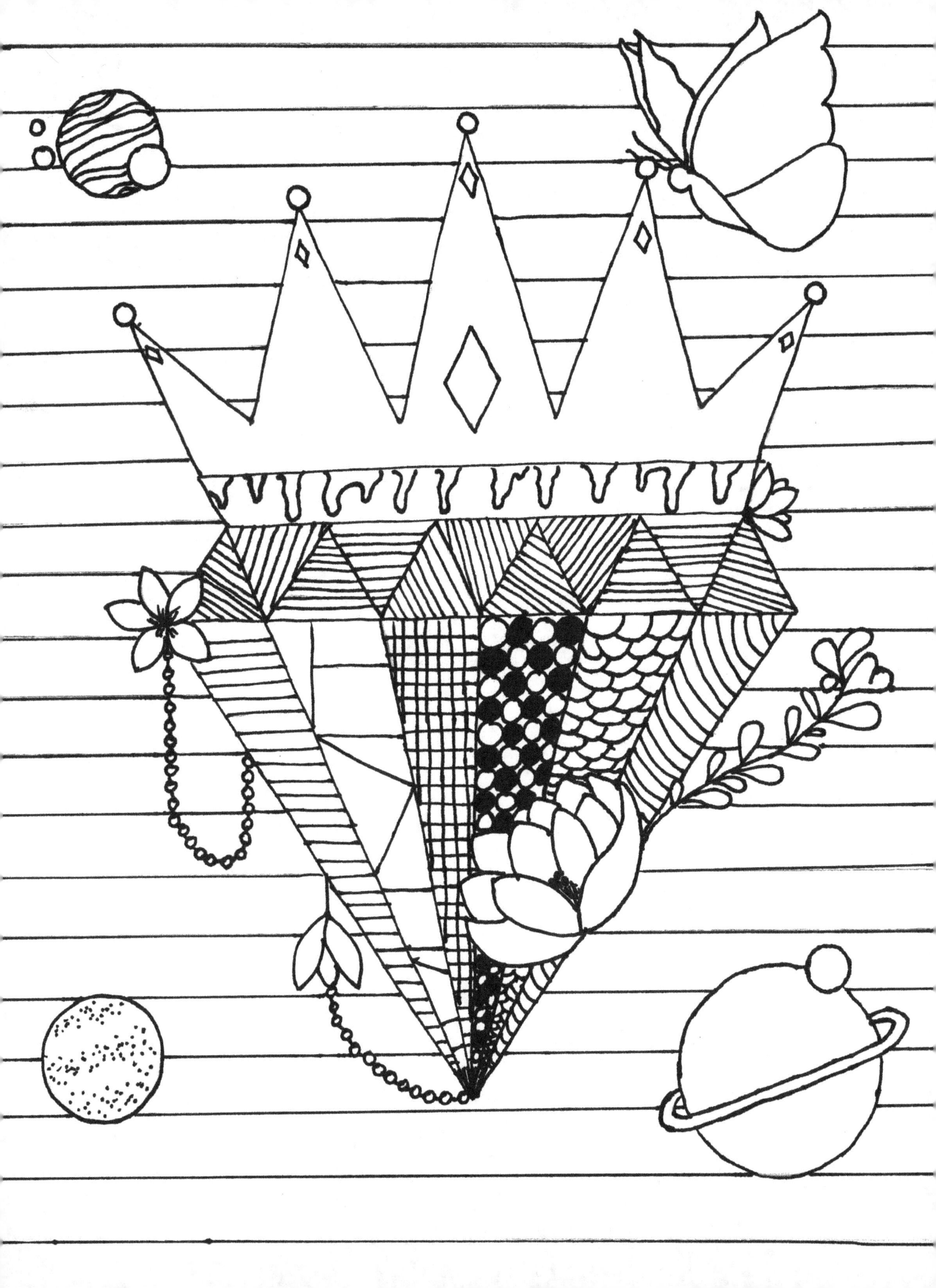

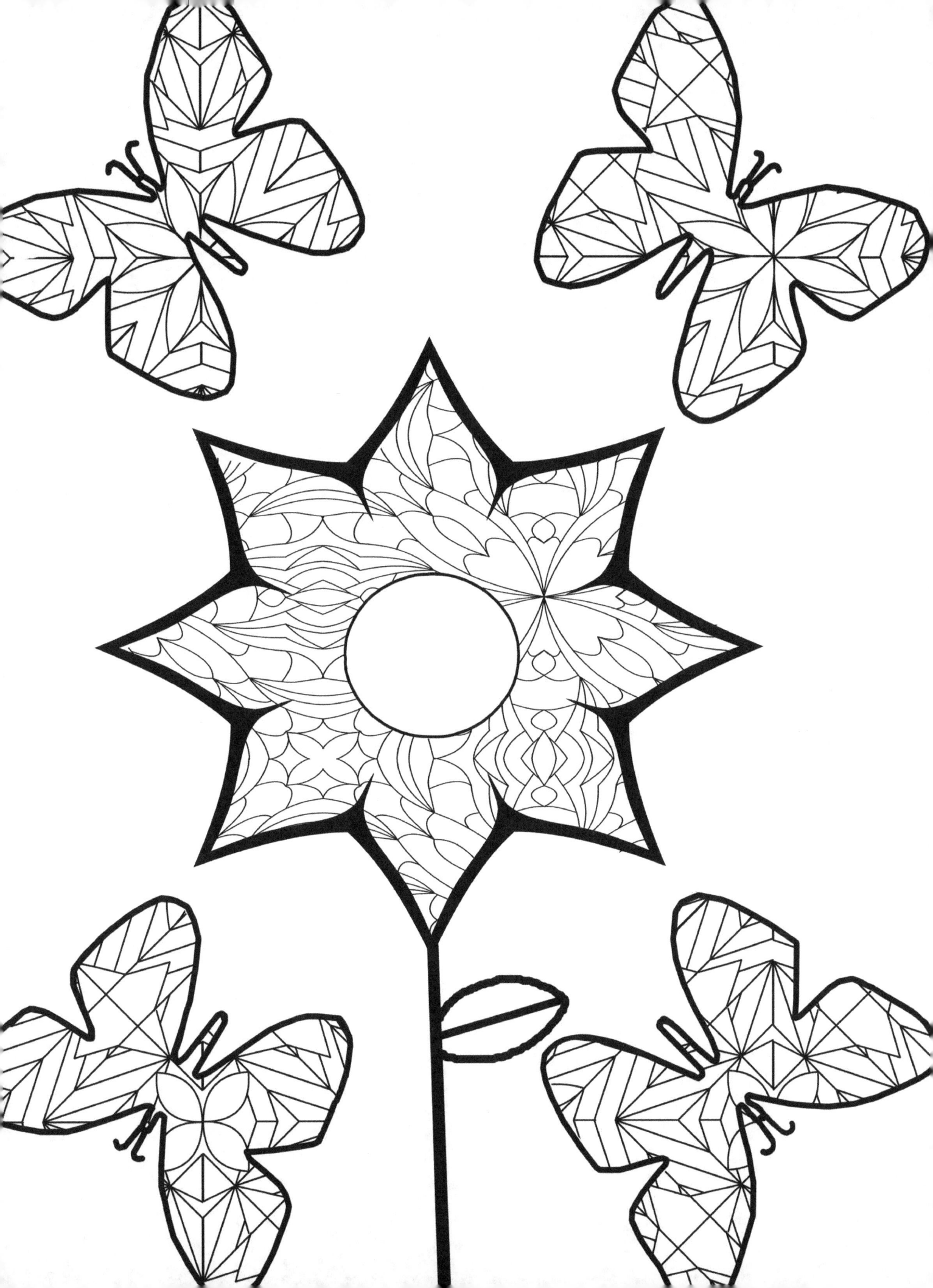

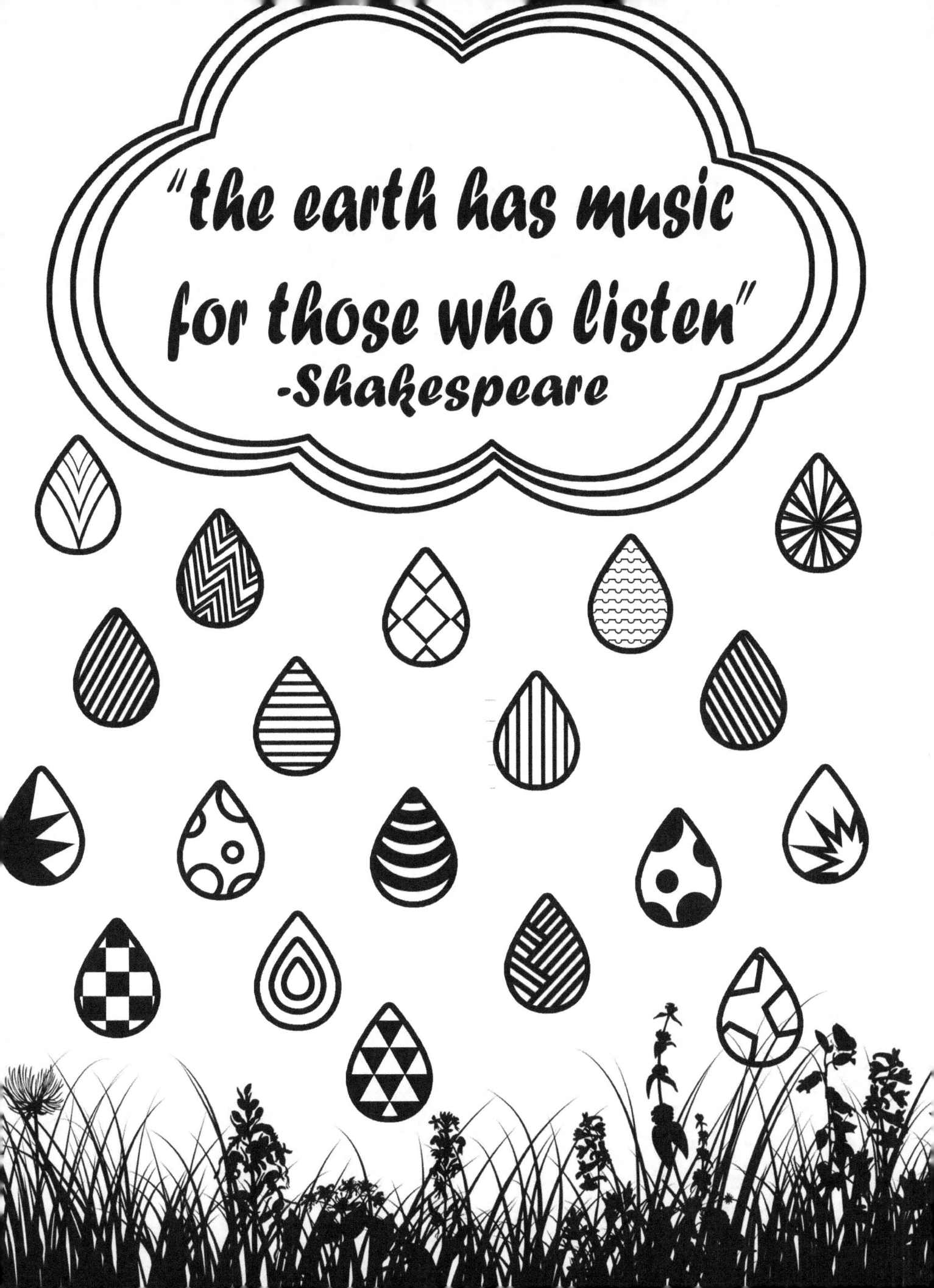

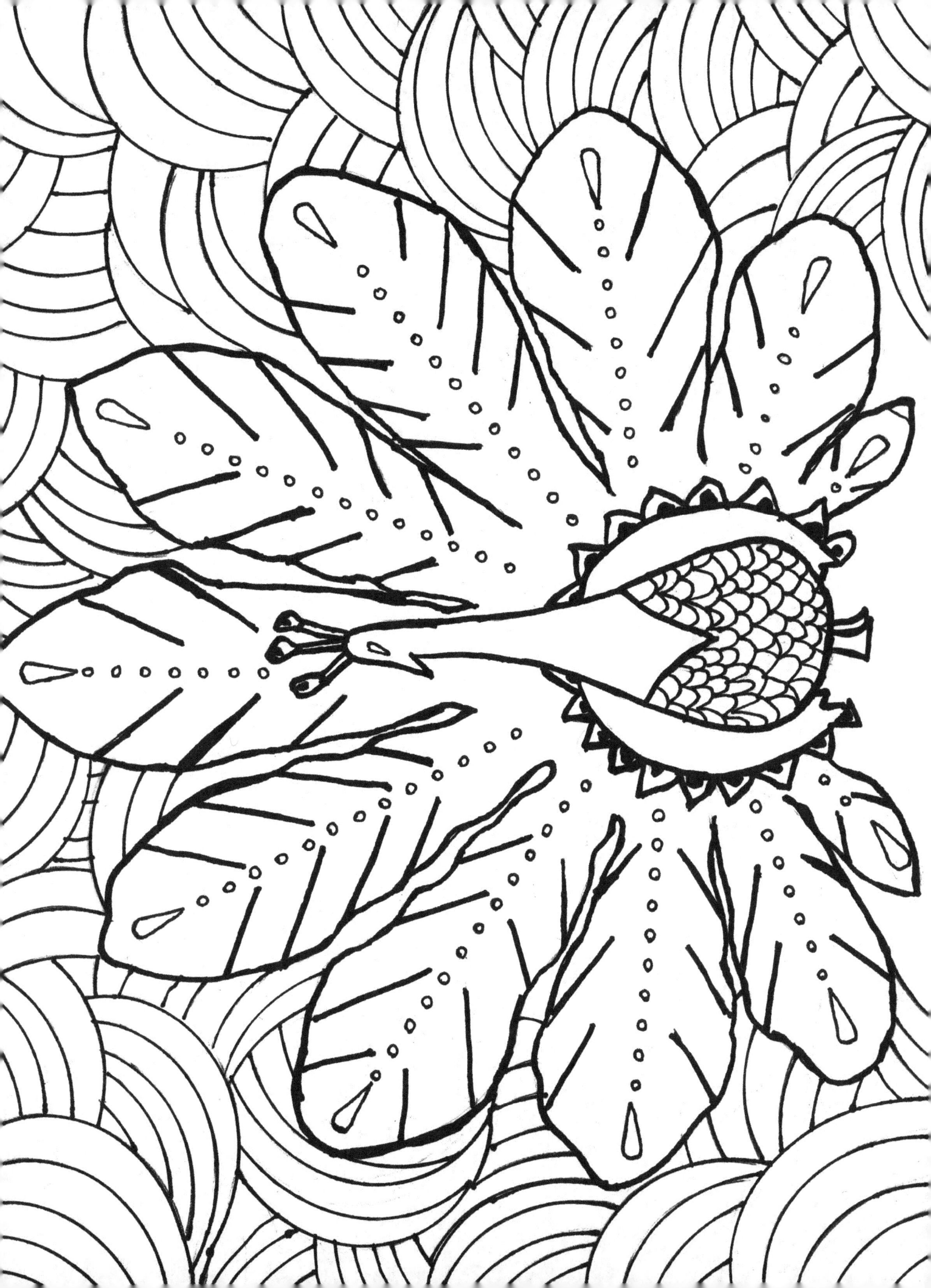

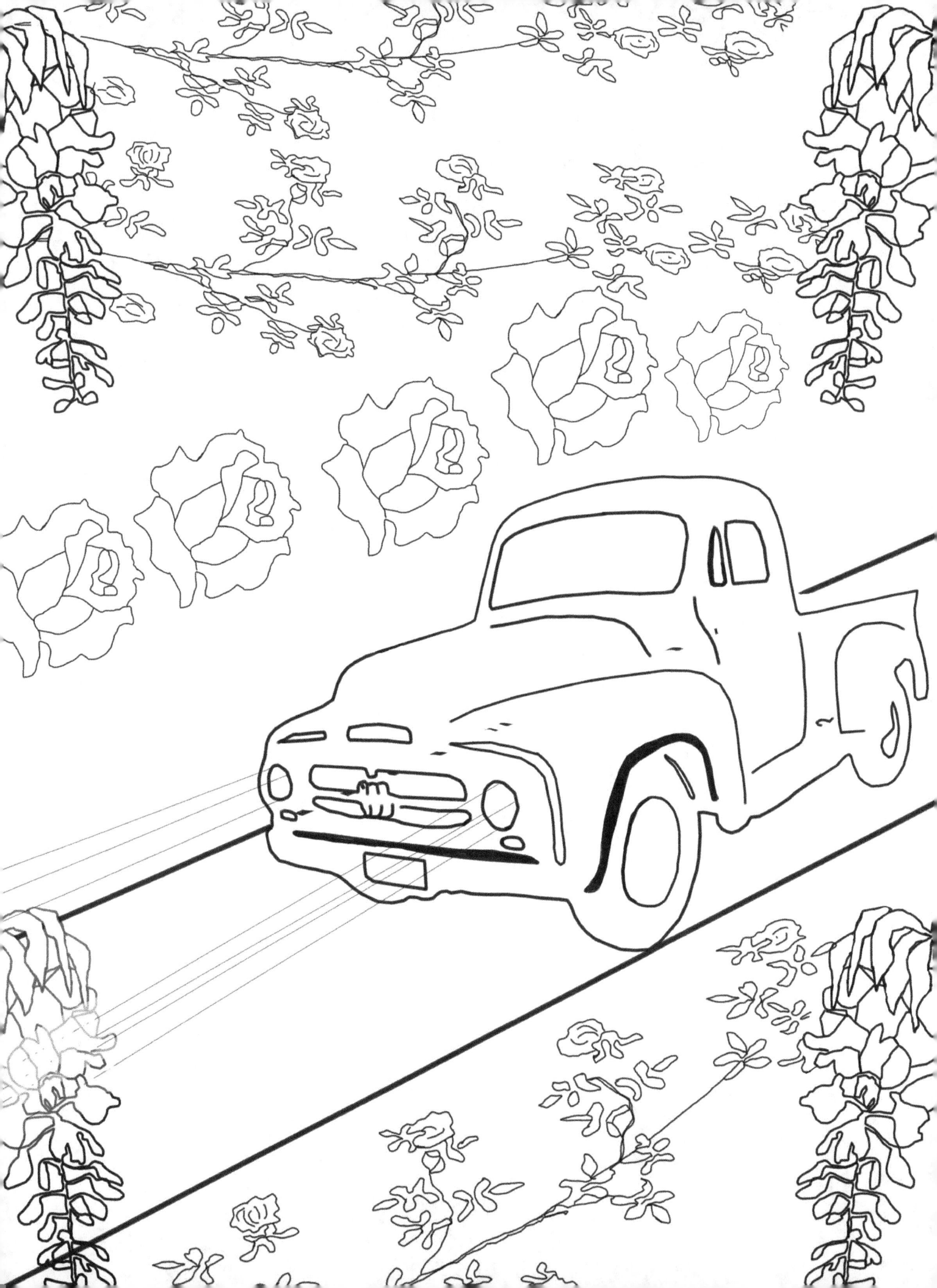

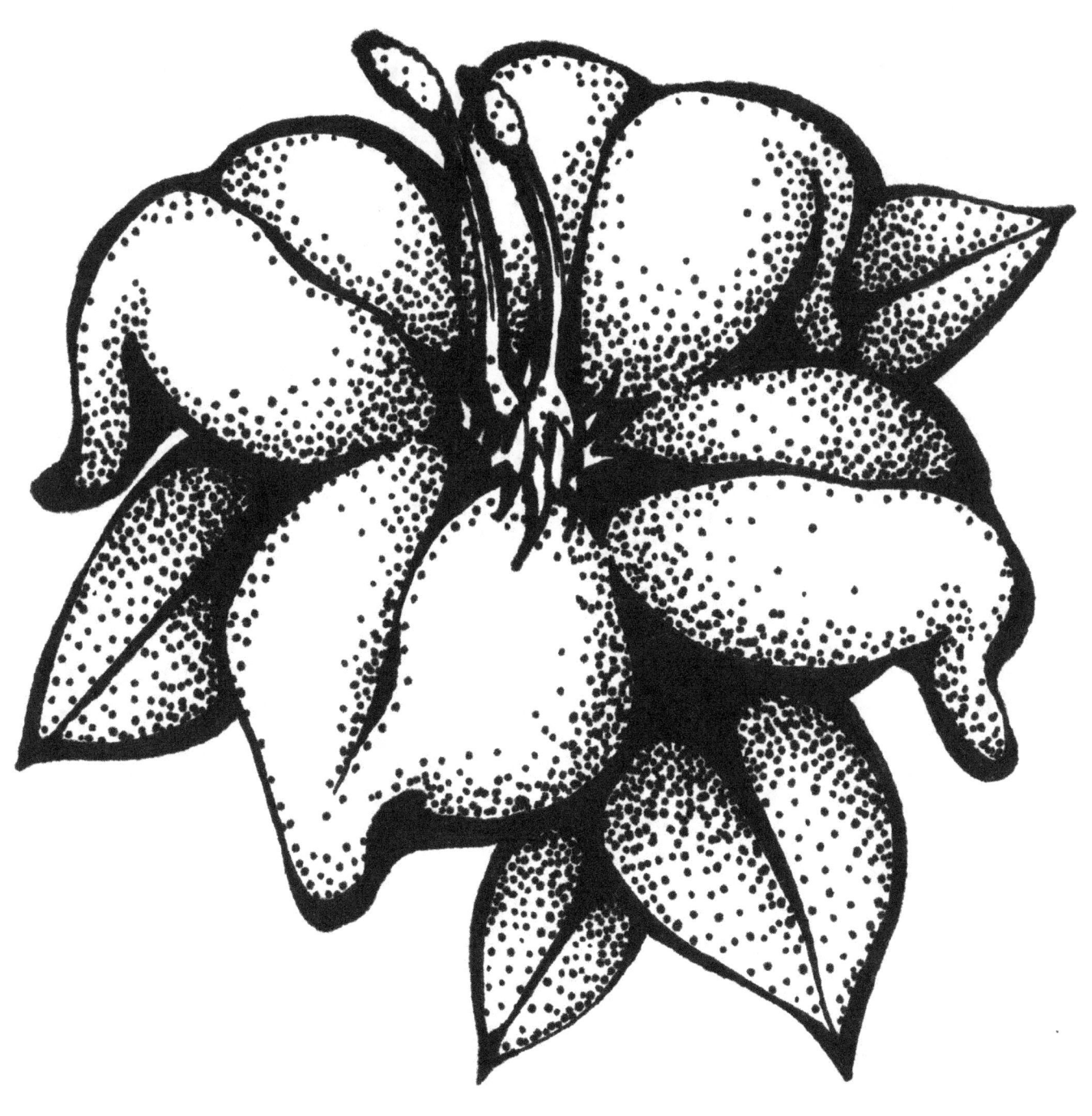

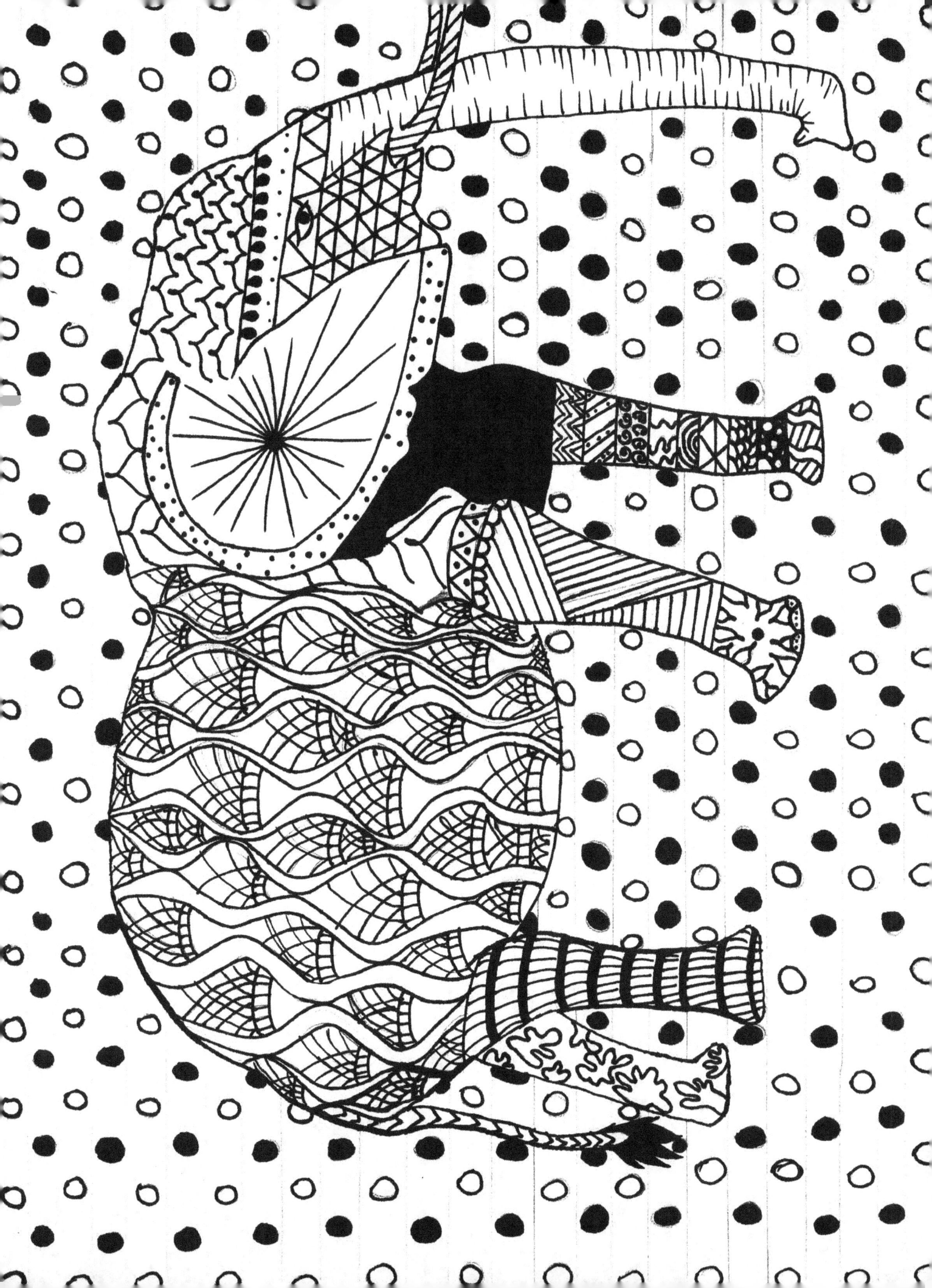

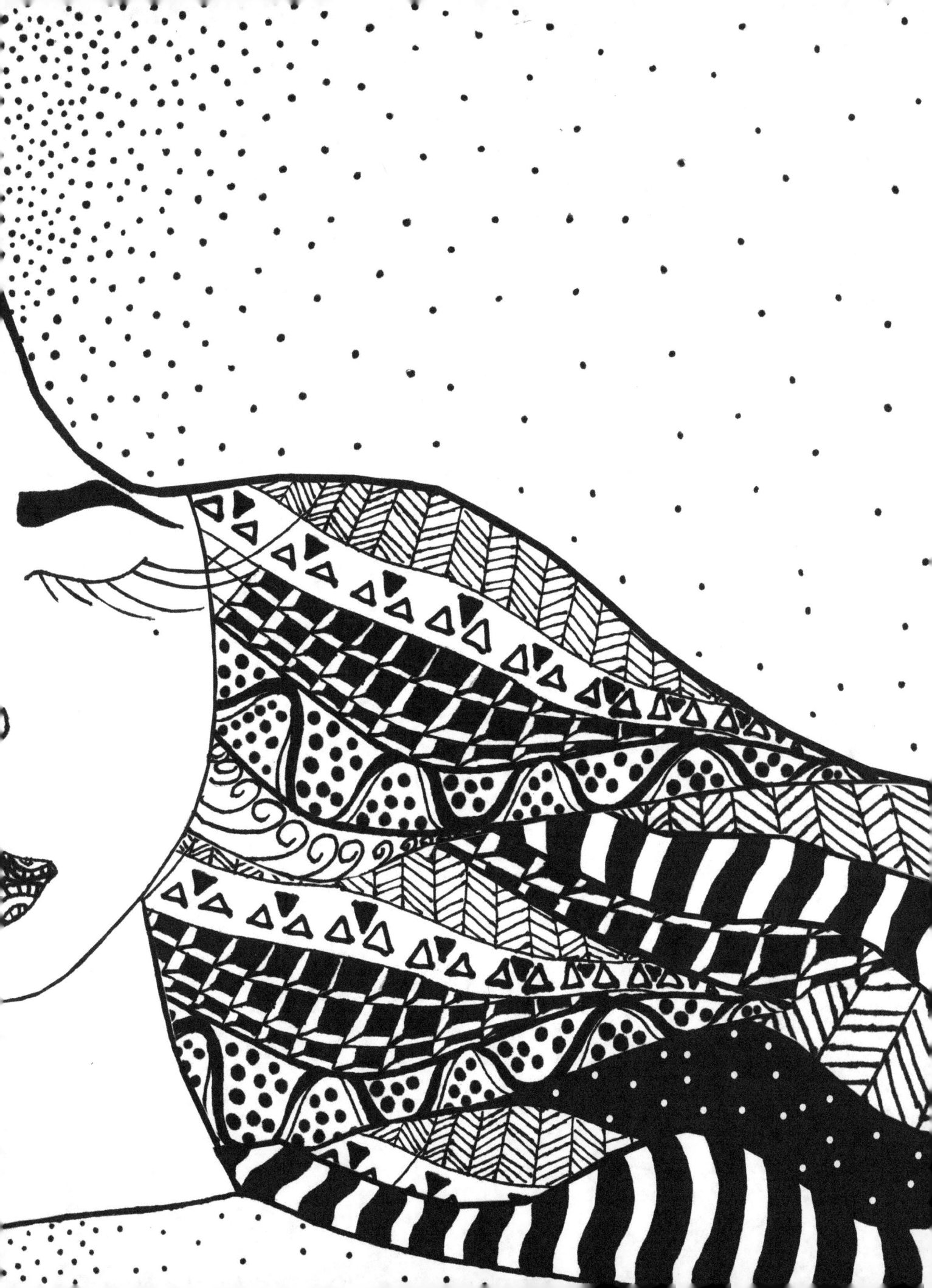

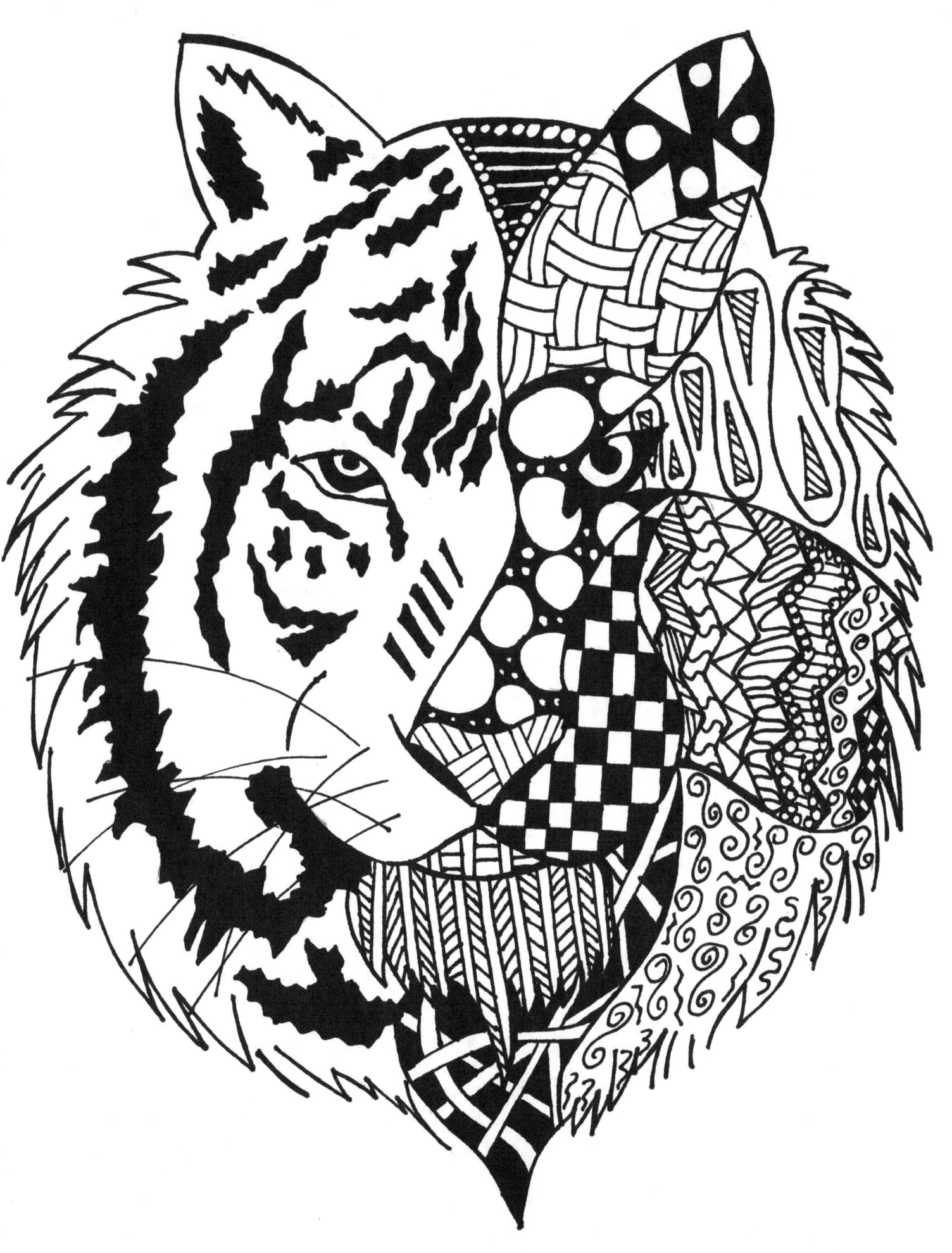

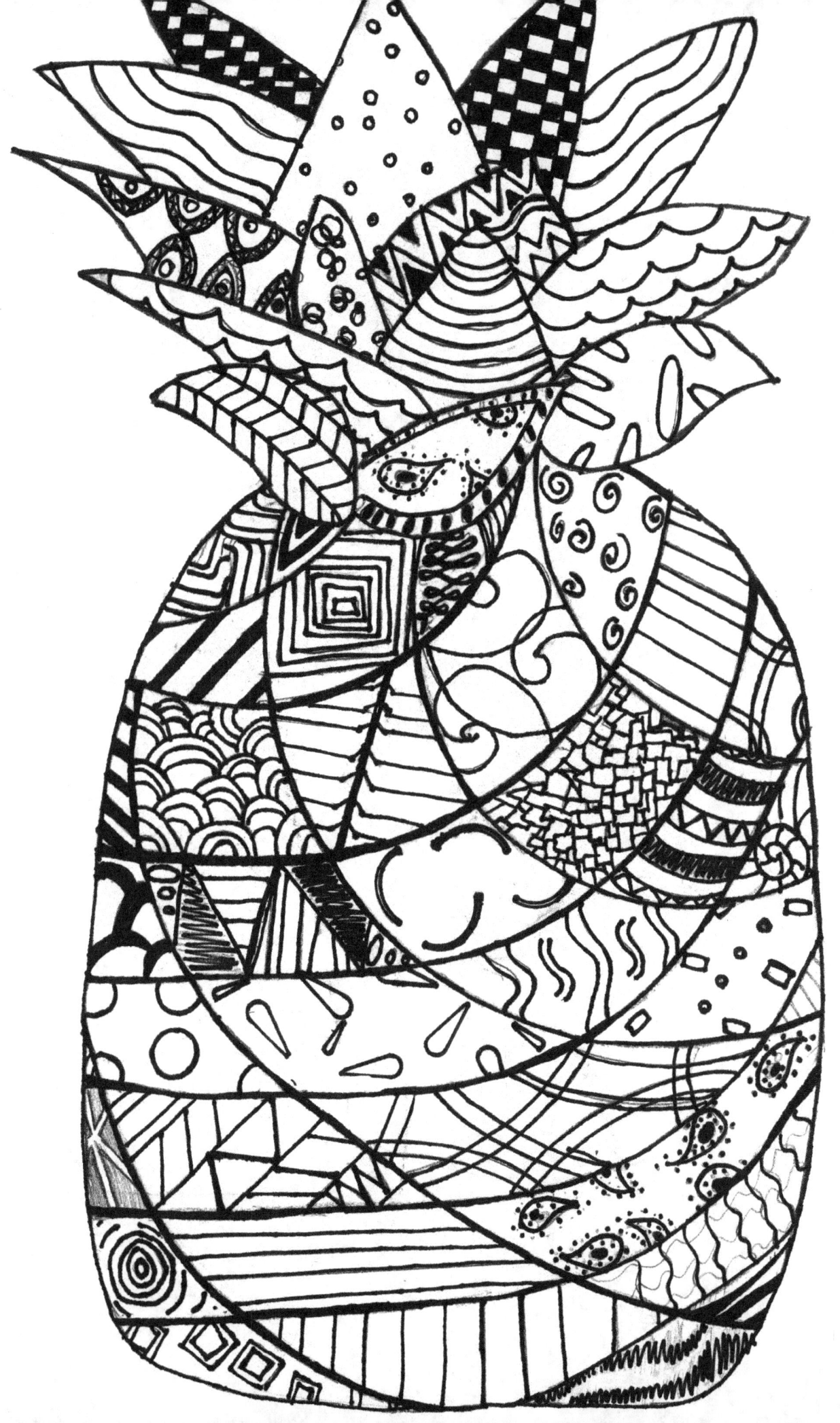

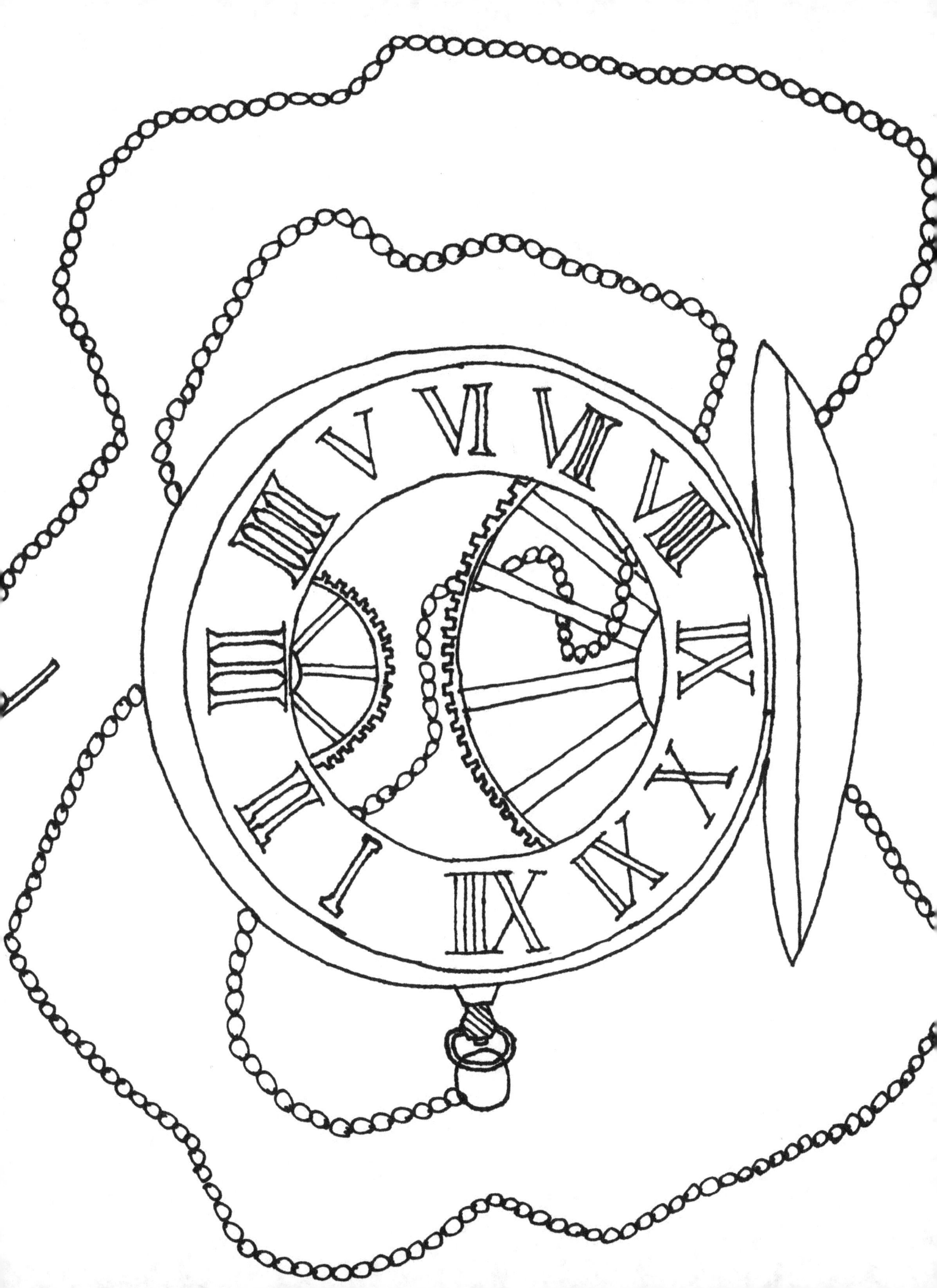

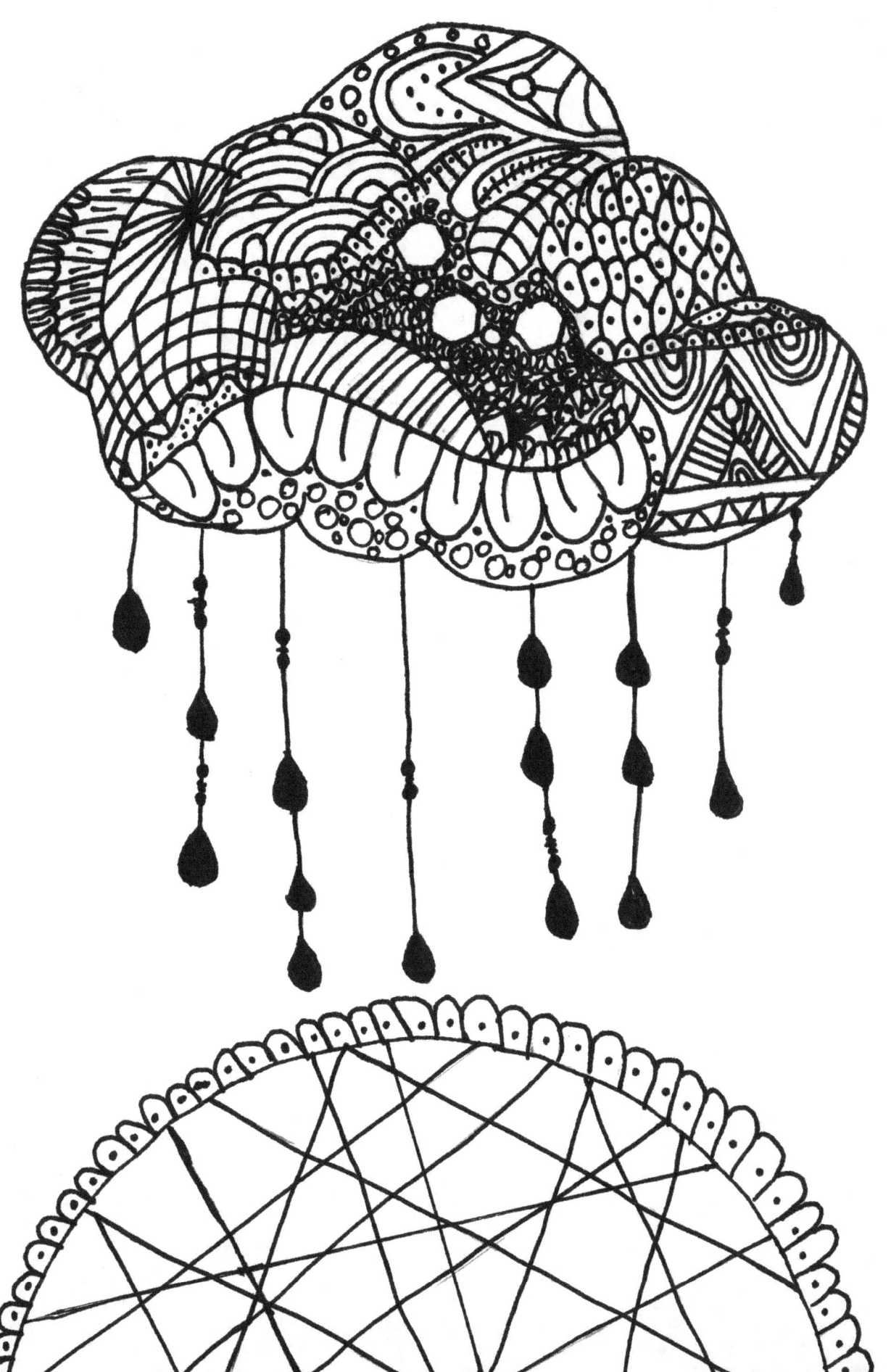

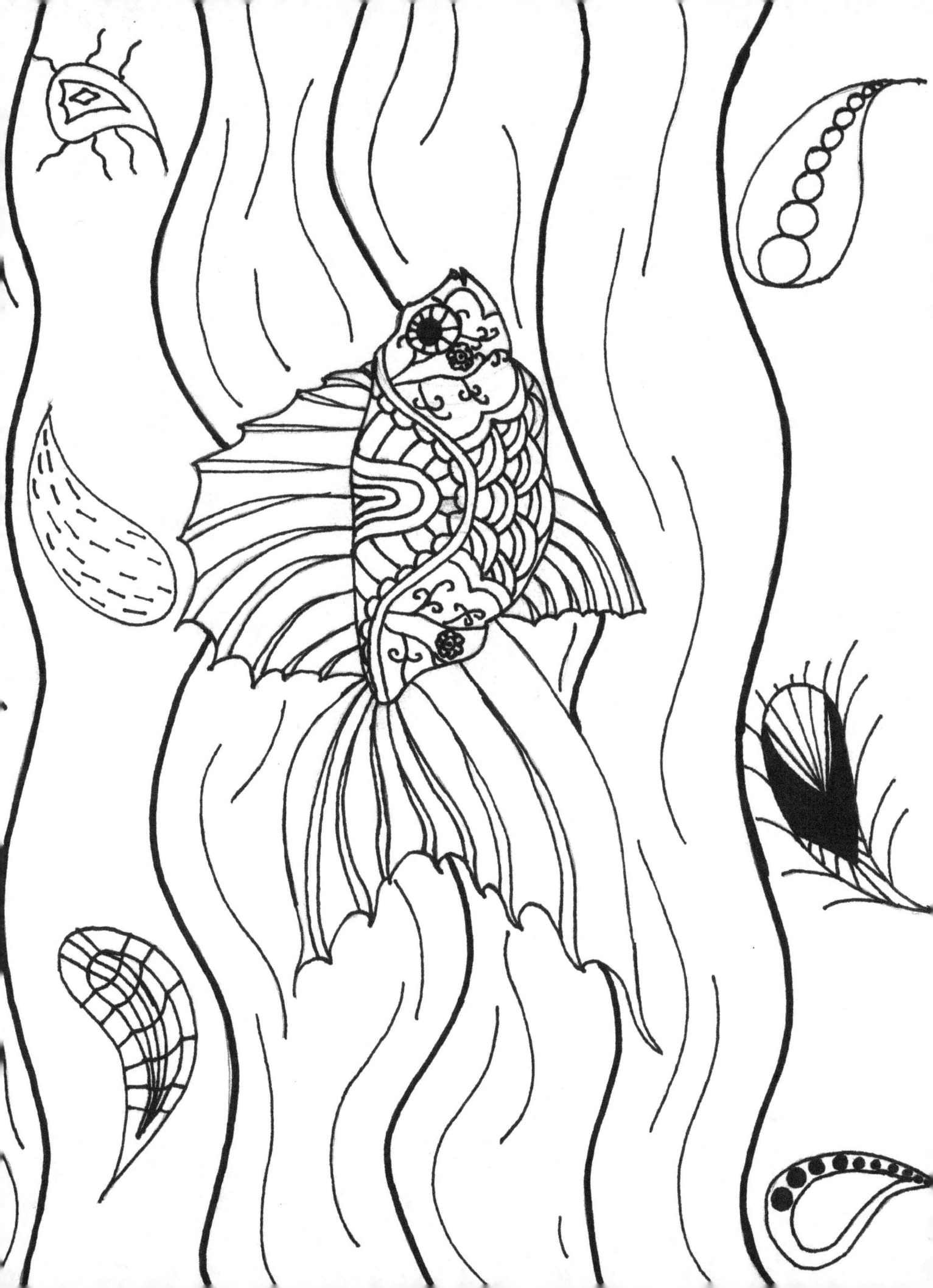

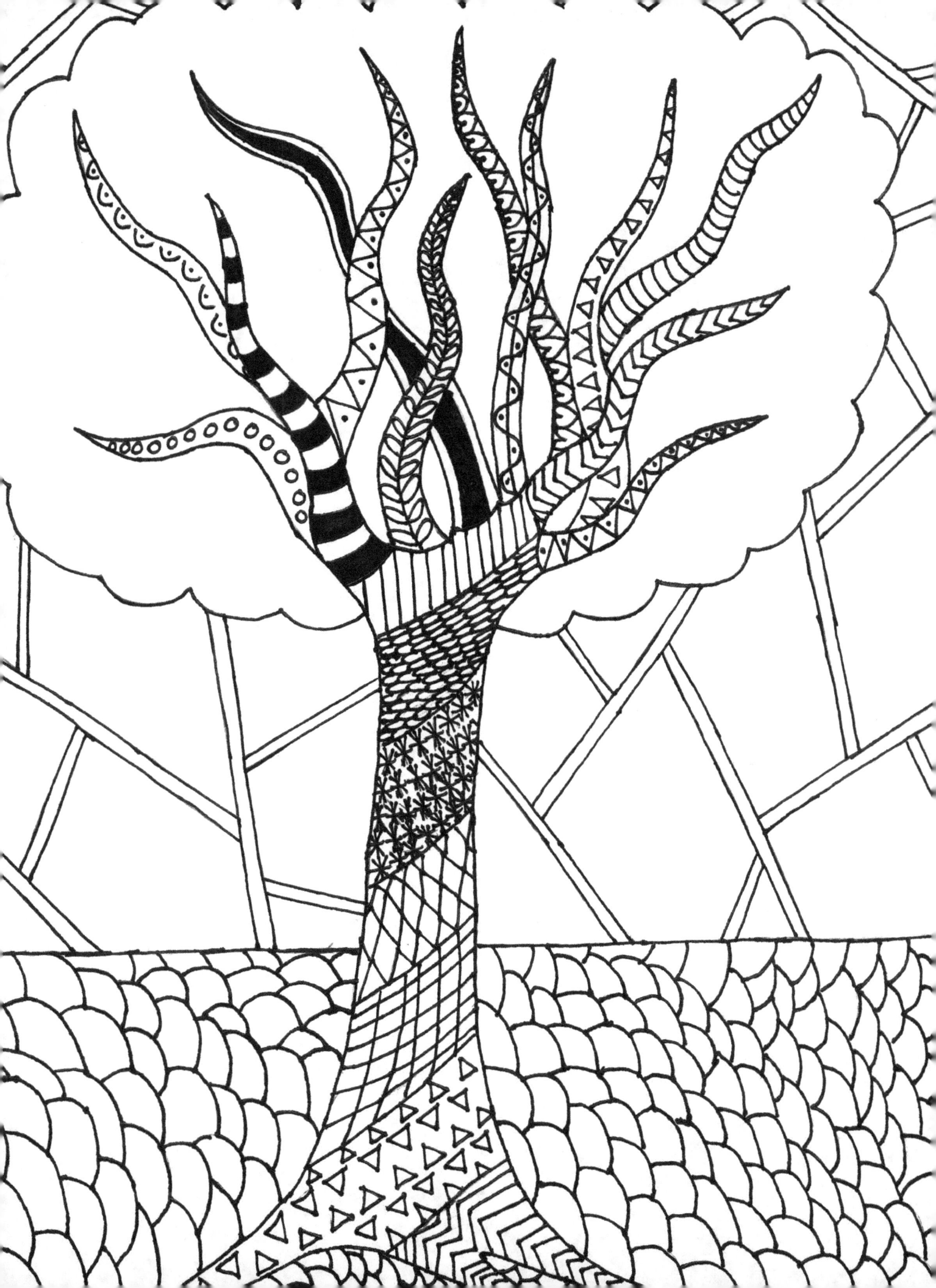

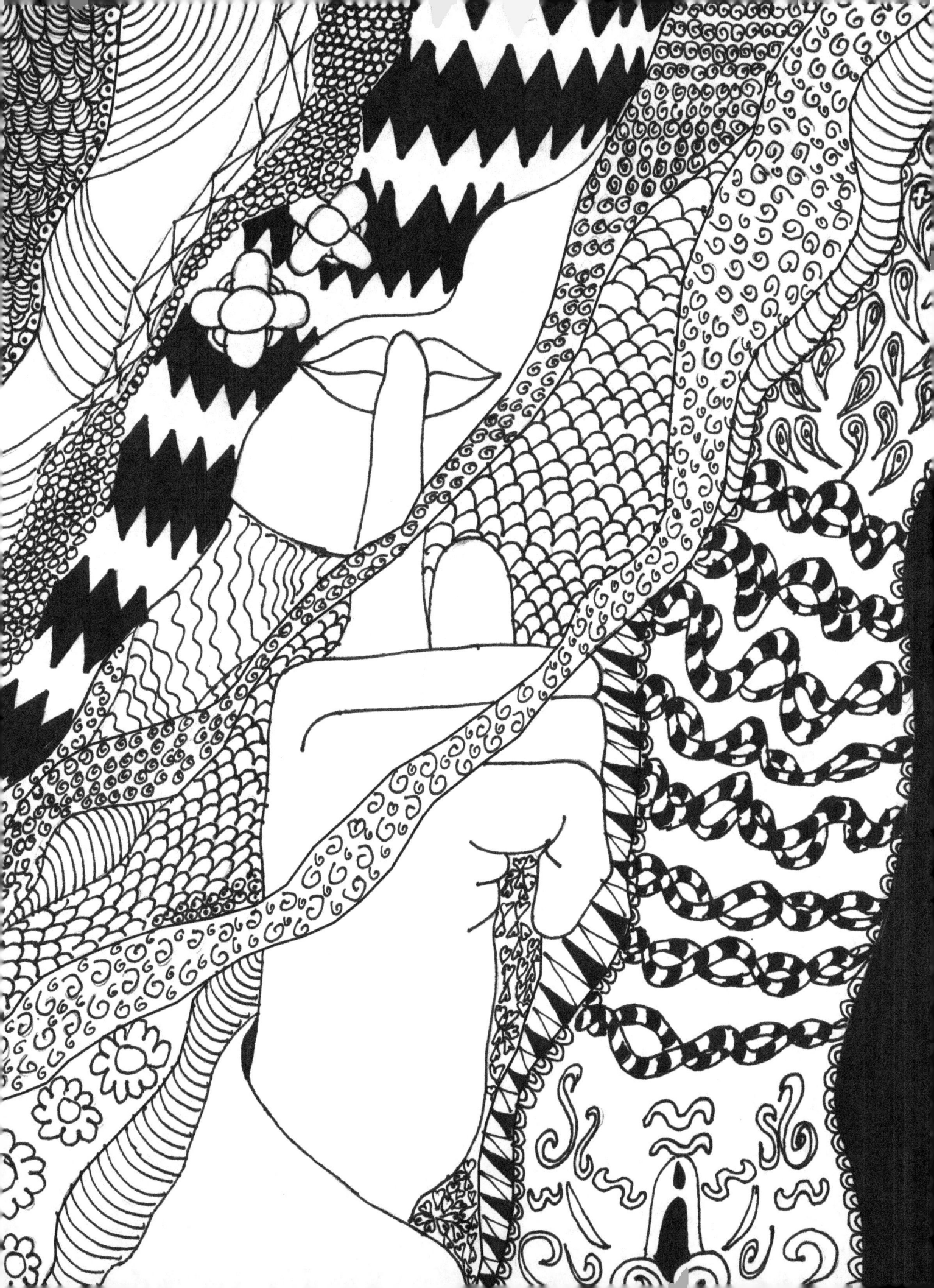

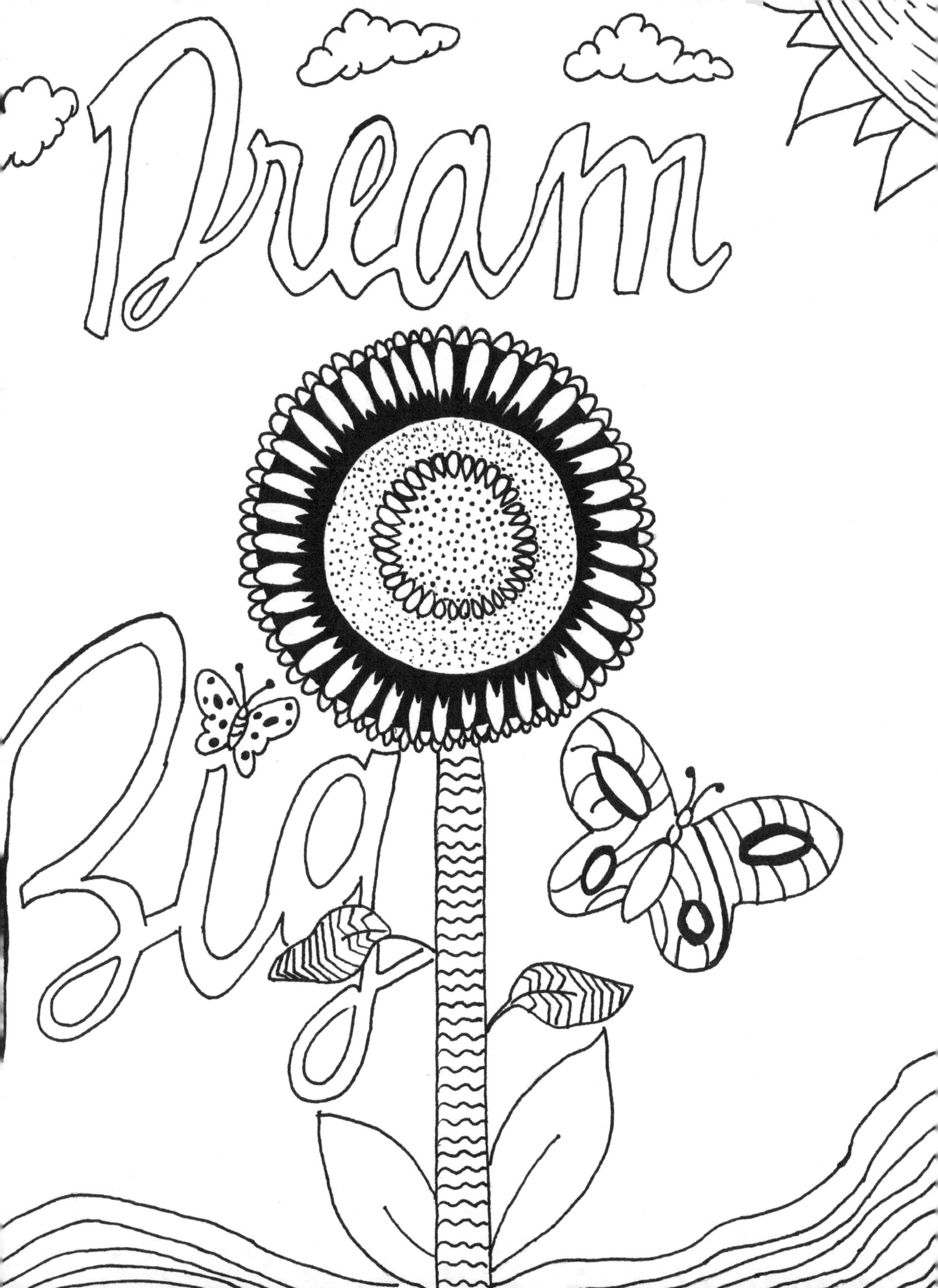

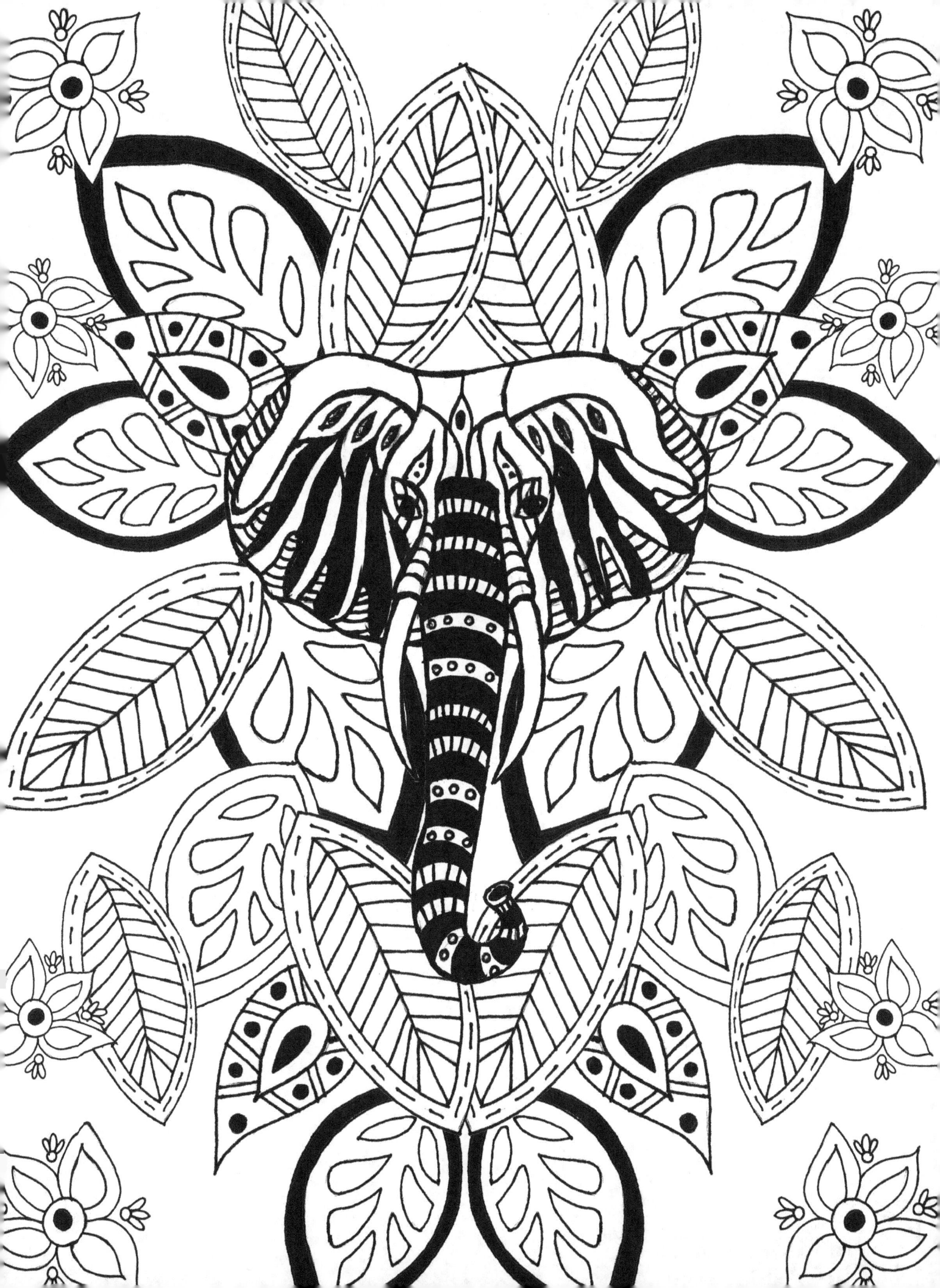